Motivation and Productivity
in Public Sector
Human Service Organizations

Motivation and Productivity in Public Sector Human Service Organizations

WILLIAM T. MARTIN

QUORUM BOOKS

NEW YORK
WESTPORT, CONNECTICUT
LONDON

Library of Congress Cataloging-in-Publication Data

Martin, William T., 1938–
  Motivation and productivity in public sector human service
organizations / William T. Martin.
    p. cm.
  Bibliography: p.
  Includes index.
  ISBN 0–89930–314–5 (lib. bdg. : alk. paper)
  1. Mental health services. 2. Mental health facilities.
3. Motivation (Psychology) 4. Government productivity. I. Title.
RA790.5.M344 1988
362.2'3'068—dc19   88–3099

British Library Cataloguing in Publication Data is available.

Library of Congress Catalog Card Number: 88–3099
ISBN: 0–89930–314–5

First published in 1988 by Quorum Books

Greenwood Press, Inc.
88 Post Road West, Westport, Connecticut 06881

Printed in the United States of America

The paper used in this book complies with the
Permanent Paper Standard issued by the National
Information Standards Organization (Z39.48–1984).

10 9 8 7 6 5 4 3 2 1

This work is dedicated to my loving and understanding wife, Patricia. Also, my daughter Monica deserves special acknowledgment for her love and understanding during the past years. Finally, to all of my associates, co-workers, and employers past who provided me with valuable insights and experiences in the human service organizations.

CONTENTS

Motivation and Productivity
in Public Sector
Human Service Organizations

1

INTRODUCTION

Motivation and productivity in public sector human service organizations (HSOs), including intermediate care facilities (ICFs) and other public and private residential facilities (PRFs) vary from a few facilities which have excellent reputations to those which are barely retaining certification, if not in a process of decertification. While it is my intent to communicate a number of positive approaches to increasing motivation and productivity of public sector facilities, the stage must be set. This stage includes some notes on historical perspectives of human services as well as the stagnation of some of our modern facilities. Policies, rules, and procedures can have the effect of decreasing motivation and productivity among employees, and there can be a certain degree of irrationality in fiscal policies which further frustrates employees.

The majority of these issues relate to the state institutions for the mentally ill and the mentally retarded. To a lesser degree, these issues thwart progress in other facilities such as residential treatment centers, nursing homes, and residential supportive organizations. General hospitals with psychiatric services and the for-profit human services corporations are probably the best managed and most oriented toward proactive motivation and productivity issues. However, it is hoped that any facility, public or private, can benefit from some of the issues presented in this book.

State-operated human service facilities can frequently be redundant with trends, fads, governmental regulation, human rights issues, vested interests, traditionalism, and lack of cost-effectiveness. There are no easy answers. Our systems are obsolete at best. For decades, systems have been plagued with bureaucratic policy. For lack of true insight into the nature of human anomaly, governments created monstrous institutions (economies of scale) which served to isolate non-average individuals in rural and/or peripheral city areas. Such behavior has been akin to the "casting out of demons" as in the Salem Witchcraft Trials, the placement of Native Americans on isolated reservations, and the persecution of those not identified with the Moral Majority.

HISTORICAL ISSUES

A review of some historical concepts sets the stage so the reader can better identify with current issues in motivation and productivity. Therapeutic efforts to eliminate mental illness and retardation problems are as old as humankind. In ancient times human treatment was an either/or condition. The motivation of practitioners in mental and physical treatment was to either banish the person from the mainstream of society or "cure" the person. During the Stone Age, the practice of *trephination* (cutting a hole in the skull to allow evil spirits to escape) was used. Even today, many primitive societies subscribe to a relationship between mental disorders and supernatural forces.

During the Greek and Roman Era (circa 400 B.C. to A.D. 476) Hippocrates and Galen advocated humane treatment of those with mental disorders. Upon the fall of the Roman Empire, the rational view of mental disorder was replaced with that of religious demonology. According to Wittenborn (1965), "modern" accounts of mental illness were also described in the Bible.

The Middle Ages (circa A.D. 476 to 1453) were noted for society's obsession with witches and that madness was considered to be the work of the Devil. The Christian work *Malleus Maleficarum* ("the witch's hammer") described signs of witches which could be identified. During the Renaissance period (circa A.D. 1400 to 1600) the practices of the Greeks and Romans reappeared. Gradually, an enlightened view of mental disorder replaced the oppressive view of the Middle Ages.

Asylums built early in the Middle Ages were designed to hold suspects and to protect society from their evil power. Compare this with our concept of modern institutions.

In 1792, soon after the French Revolution, Philippe Pinel was placed in charge of an asylum for the insane in Paris. He tried an experiment. He removed the shackles of the insane and began treating them with kindness. His reforms were successful. Mental institutions continued to be reformed during the eighteenth and nineteenth centuries, but little was known about mental disorders. Patients were put together in large groups in large institutions, and individualized treatment had yet to be discovered as we know it today. Dorothea Dix (1802–1887) also helped to establish humane, professionally run hospitals.

Prior to the nineteenth century, persons suffering from significant mental and emotional problems were generally considered to be hopelessly beyond the realm of rehabilitation (as we know it today); no concerted attempts were really made to treat them (Tredgold, 1952). In the area of mental retardation, Heiser and Wolman (1965) described the work of the French educationalist Itard in 1801. The classic case, the "wild boy of Aveyron," was described. Itard found this boy in 1798, living like a wild animal in the forest. Itard's colleague, Pinel, examined the boy and concluded that he was an idiot without hope of being educated.

Since about 1800, three periods in treatment were noted. The first was known as the "moral-treatment" era (circa 1817 until the Civil War in the United States). During this period, many hospitals were erected for individuals who were emotionally, behaviorally, and mentally different from the masses. The superintendent was noted to have played an important role, knowing every patient, and living on the grounds (Greenblatt and Levinson, 1965). Charles Dickens (1842) described an institution in South Boston (Boston State Hospital): "Every patient in this asylum sits down to dinner every day with a knife and fork; and in the midst of them sits the gentleman [superintendent]. The patients worked, read, played, and exercised. In the labour department, every patient is as freely trusted with the tools of his trade as if he were a sane man."

This description can be compared with current models of active treatment. We continue to take a circular route in human services while at the same time making some progress. For example, decades ago mentally ill and mentally retarded patients were assigned work details on the farms, gardens, and dairies. (I will use the term "patient" in this book to refer to all categories of clients, residents, and patients since several types of facilities, such as general hospitals, nursing homes, and others appropriately use the term.) Then, we went to "humane treatment" whereby our patients did not do any work and generally sat on the wards to vegetate in the absence of active treatment. In the past twenty years or so we have rediscovered such innovative techniques as "horticulture therapy," which has been found to be a rather effective form of therapy for some of the higher-functioning patients. Some facilities that have used horticulture therapy in modern times have included the Menninger Foundation, the Kansas Elks Training Center, the Melwood Horticulture Training Center, and some Veterans Administration (VA) hospitals.

The second period involved a decline of the moral-treatment era and occurred from about the Civil War until the early part of the twentieth century. As the mental hospitals became larger, more numerous, and composed of chronic patients, moral treatment was abandoned. Society was only mildly interested in patient welfare and was content to have these outcasts separated from the mainstream of the community.

Around 1925, active care for the institutionalized patient began to be reimplemented. With the advent of insulin and other convulsive therapies in the 1930s, the patient was again "treated." During World War II, new insight was gained into the treatment and rehabilitation of psychiatric patients. The value of group therapy and testing was realized (though the testing movement had gained momentum during World War I). Psychoactive drugs made their debut in 1955 with the introduction of the first major tranquilizer. In 1955, Congress passed the Mental Health Study Act which directed a Joint Commission to make recommendations for a national mental health program. Community mental health centers, under President Kennedy's administration, gained significant impetus in 1963 (Braceland, 1966). The institutional concept was beginning to decline and massive efforts to discharge patients began about 1963, continuing through the present.

According to the National Institute of Mental Health (NIMH, 1985), over 450 psychiatric hospitals were listed. The NIMH (1983) reported about 923 non-federal general hospital psychiatric services (1978 data) present in the United States. Other figures included Veterans Administration psychiatric services (N = 136); federally funded clinics (N = 691); residential treatments centers for emotionally disturbed children (N = 368); and freestanding psychiatric outpatient clinics (N = 1,053). Between about 1970 and 1980 there was a 62 percent decrease in inpatient beds at state and county mental hospitals. At the same time, there was about a 166 percent increase in the number of day treatment services being provided.

The NIMH (1983) also reported that the total number of facilities which provided mental health services increased from about 3,005 in 1970 to about 3,727 in 1980; state and county mental hospitals evidenced a decrease in the number of facilities. The number of facilities which provided services in the inpatient setting increased about 46 percent between 1970 and 1980 but the number of beds decreased by about 48 percent. General hospitals, community mental health centers, and residential treatment centers evidenced a significant increase in the number of facilities; however, these increases have failed to accommodate the patients discharged from the institutions. Facilities treating substance abusers have increased in number during this decade.

The United States Bureau of the Census (Bureau, 1985) reported that there were about 14,605 private ICFs serving the mentally retarded with about 364 being state operated. In 1982 there were about 3,018 drug abuse treatment units and 6,116 general hospitals, with about 23,065 nursing and related facilities being reported in 1980. In 1982 there were about 251,000 employees serving about 157,000 patients in psychiatric hospitals. In 1980 it was reported that only about 918,000 employees were serving some 1,329,000 patients in nursing homes. In psychiatric hospitals, the number of employees per 100 patients rose from about 35 in 1960 to about 167 in 1982. Among state and private residential facilities serving the mentally retarded, the average daily census decreased from about 447 in 1960 to about 338 in 1982. In terms of programs and facilities serving mentally disordered offenders, the NIMH (1986) reported about 180 facilities serving adult and juvenile individuals. These ranged from minimum to maximum security facilities.

Curtis (1986) noted that the census of psychiatric facilities was at a peak in 1955 (when major tranquilizers were introduced); mental retardation facilities displayed their peak population about 1970. Around 1984, health care was said to be the nation's third largest industry (Davis, 1984). With the trend toward deinstitutionalization continuing, the Mental Retardation Facilities and Community Mental Health Centers Construction Act also shifted the focus of mental health care from state institutions to local communities. Mental illness became an issue of "social deviance" with mental retardation being one of "developmental disability," a learning problem. But deinstitutionalization has not been without problems. In New York City, it has been estimated that about 30 to 60 percent of the homeless were mentally disabled. Similar figures can be observed in other large cities, including Denver, Los Angeles, Dallas, and Chicago.

For practical purposes, the issues of motivation and productivity did not really begin to be an important concern in American business settings until the findings of the Hawthorne studies were published (Roethlisberger and Dickson, 1939). More on this later.

THE PUBLIC SERVICE FACILITY CRISIS

A crisis, like stress, is a relative thing. What may be a crisis to one person may not be so to another. Human service organizations (HSOs) are no exception. Institutions for the so-called insane and mentally defective have been in a state of alternate reform and backsliding since the Middle Ages. And this crisis did not begin to become significantly stabilized and proactive until about 1955, with the advent of major tranquilizing drugs. Deinstitutionalization movements of the 1960s and 1970s promoted yet other crises in treatment. We can probably thank people of the baby-boom generation for aggressively questioning the status of our current concepts in institutional treatment. This was (and is) a generation of self-realization, anti-conventionalism, and speaking out about the alleged injustices of society and bureaucracies. It was also an era of landmark and precedent-setting Supreme Court decisions in the area of human rights, discrimination, and other social reform. Unfortunately, the mass exodus of institutionalized patients was analogous to a mass parole of tenured prison inmates. We advocated and accomplished the release of patients from the institutions; unfortunately, we were a touch remiss in ensuring that these individuals were prepared to meet the demands of a rapidly changing, post-industrial society.

Issues of public policy, legislation, and related reforms will not be dwelled on here. The reader will find adequate treatment of these matters in the works of Thaw and Cuvo (1986); Favell, Favell, Riddle, and Risley (1984), and others.

With continuing attention to a myriad of human mental and physical problems (along with the issue of deinstitutionalization), increased burdens are placed upon facility administrators and caregivers. The NIMH (1985) listed a number of HSO categories. These were: outpatient mental health clinics, psychiatric hospitals, residential treatment centers, mental health day/night facilities, multiservice mental health organizations, general hospitals with separate psychiatric services, residential treatment organizations, and residential supportive organizations. Excluded in their survey were mental retardation and developmental disability, sheltered workshops, vocational rehabilitation agencies, day training and schools, private outpatient, nursing homes, emergency psychiatric service, and VA psychiatric facilities. In this book, I will use the designation "HSO" to refer to these organizations, facilities, and agencies in general. Specific designations will be used as appropriate.

The scope of these various HSOs and their services involves numerous compliances with federal standards in terms of service delivery. The Health Care Finance Administration (HCFA) has been one especially active monitoring agency in the regulation and administration of Title XIX funding, for facilities serving the mentally retarded, general hospitals, and others. Another agency, the Council for Accreditation of Rehabilitation Facilities (CARF), causes similar excitement for administrators of these agencies. Compliance with these (and other) regulations is no mean task. Facilities are continually inoculated with rules, regulations, and mandates which do not always interface with available fiscal and human resources. With increased governmental regulation, and concomitant paperwork, caregivers have frequently been inadvertently forced to subordinate proactive treatment to the ever-increasing paperwork requirements. It becomes a Catch–22 situation. Insufficient funds are provided by state legislatures for the ultimate compliance with Title XIX regulations; if you don't comply, you don't get the money (or they close you down).

Thaw, Benjamin, and Cuvo (1986) stated that public residential facilities (PRFs) were experiencing "unmanageable change and unmanaged innovation" (p. 168). They noted that the unit management system of service delivery (for residential facilities serving the mentally retarded) was one of the best ways to manage. However, this system can create additional problems: former professionals have been assigned to unit management positions with little formal training in the area of administration.

PRFs are in a crisis of recovering from past injustices to patients. The institutions are not the most glamorous places in which to work and recruiting quality employees is difficult. The bureaucratic system often prevents the removal of inefficient, and non-advocate employees from our institutions due to issues of seniority and tenure (and perhaps inadequate labor pools). Productivity has suffered and we have moved from institutionalized patients to an era of rapid change and some institutionalized staff.

While there are many unanswered questions in regard to the best and most productive form of treatment, habilitation, and rehabilitation for patients in institutions, only a few institutions have the status of being research facilities. *Research* has become an obscene word among some individuals. The concept that "humane treatment and research don't mix" seems to prevail in the minds of some opponents. On the other hand, a few selected institutions advocate and are doing research. What better setting to study and foster knowledge and innovation in our institutions than in the institution itself? To some, the word *research* connotes a form of black-box, rat-running model. To others, the meaning is one of anti–human rights. There must be a happy compromise somewhere. We need to find additional solutions through the process of scientific inquiry. If we all pooled our intellect and resources and worked together, we might solve some of our own problems. As McNamara (1986) stressed, there was an urgent need to expand our efforts in applied research.

Service delivery systems have evolved from the chains and shackles of Bedlam to psychoactive drugs and other special treatment procedures. In both psychiatric and mental retardation facilities we still do not have the answers. But improvements are continually being made. Deinstitutionalization continues. Community-based and outpatient facilities continue to emerge. The public is becoming more aware of the early signs of human dysfunction and striving to take appropriate prophylactic action. Support groups and faddish therapies are found in abundance.

Psychiatric hospitals, mental retardation facilities, and related residential facilities continue to work toward improving treatment efficacy and finding better answers, in spite of the federal regulations and institutional traditions.

THE MOTIVATION AND PRODUCTIVITY ISSUE

For centuries, institutions had the luxury of economics of scale, no federal regulations, and simple goals of containment and order. Treatment, when it occurred, was primarily that needed to segregate the abnormal from the mainstream of society and to keep order among the patients. Even as late as the twentieth century, there was the issue of a *good* patient—one who was properly controlled with such therapies as insulin shock, electroconvulsive shock, an occasional prefrontal lobotomy, straitjackets, hydrotherapy, work therapy, and drug therapy. (Some of these therapies are still being used.) Staff ratios were low. Economies of scale were common. Massive stone buildings—each with two to four floors and large open rooms—were common. There are still a number of these institutions presently being used in the United

States. In fact, I visited some in 1985 and 1986 which were still operational. One was like some edifice built during the Roman Empire! Massive granite and marble buildings. Excellent for corralling patients.

When you only had one or two attendants for 50, 100, or 150 patients, aversive treatments were essential. For reasons of safety, one could not have aggression and other forms of chaos on the ward. Since staff were primarily concerned with maintaining order on the wards, administration was less concerned with staff who were altruistic, motivated, and productive—at least from the standpoint of proactive treatment paradigms.

In the author's site visits to a number of inpatient and outpatient psychiatric and mental retardation facilities in the Midwest, Great Plains, and South over the past twenty years, the prolific and colorful tales of the old days have been revealing. In the psychiatric hospitals, either the use of aversive treatment or the lack of humane treatment was common, even during the period between World War II and 1975. With facilities serving the mentally retarded, there have been accounts of similar treatment as late as the 1980s. Additionally, it is not uncommon to find direct-care workers (aides) who have worked in such facilities as long as twenty, thirty, or forty years whose earlier attitudes toward treatment have held on.

The transition from custodial, herding, and control forms of intervention to the current modalities of active treatment has not been without casualties. Direct-care workers who were from the "old school" have not always adjusted well to the new demands of active treatment, accountability, less reliance upon use of drugs, and a constant barrage of rules, regulations, and system change. As such, motivations have often been of a survival nature, with productivity reaching only the level being perceived as adequate to keep one's job.

Professionals, too, have had their frustrations. Once considered experts in a mystical world of discipline jargon and generally detached from the day-to-day interactions with the patients, they are increasingly being asked to participate in more and more active forms of treatment and to be significantly more accountable for their actions. The author recalls his internship as a psychologist at a psychiatric facility in the late 1960s. The interns had considerable freedom in testing and therapy. Even after the internship, those who remained at the facility generally had a free hand at scheduling their day, engaging in research, and participating in team meetings and treatment as they wanted. There were few administrative demands other than processing minimal paperwork and trying not to disrupt the flow of the bureaucracy. Now, professionals working in PRFs rarely have time to carry out the legal mandates of their jobs, much less the luxury of a casual therapeutic schedule. Interdisciplinary teams have increased in significance, with the group process often overriding the biases of the individual practitioner. To further complicate the smooth functioning of such facilities, threat of (or actual) decertification, budgetary constraints and a myriad of federal regulations can distort and burden organizational systems, especially those terminally constipated with the status quo.

The general plan of this book is to address various issues which relate to motivation and productivity among direct-care and professional employees in public sector HSOs. The issues of job satisfaction, commitment, attitudes, and barriers to motivation and productivity are addressed. While books that have addressed motivation and productivity in the business and industry setting, educational settings, and the human service setting have made a significant contribution to our fund of knowledge, they generally do not address a marriage of such principles. There are lessons to be learned from business and industry in the areas of motivation, productivity, human factors, employee training, and employee recruitment, selection, and placement. The only difference in the management of people is that people are managed a little differently, based upon the product or service being delivered.

HSOs are frequently not cost-effective. While they should incorporate a certain economy of scale, they should also try to learn some lessons from business and industry, including some of the "productivity through people" issues described by Peters and Waterman (1982). One example of non–cost effectiveness in state institutions is the frequent lack of efficient clerical personnel. It is not unusual for professional employees to have to do their own typing and word processing in order to meet deadlines for reports. I had much rather see psychologists, social workers, QMRPs (qualified mental retardation professionals), or registered nurses doing their specialized jobs than having to play games with administration over inadequate clerical support.

2

SERVICE DELIVERY SYSTEMS AND THE BUREAUCRACY

A bureaucracy is but one form of organizational structure. Mintzberg (1979, 1981) suggested five structures of organizations. The *simple structure* was composed of central control (as in a small business, owner-employee configuration), with middle management usually absent. In a *machine bureaucracy*, a hierarchy of control was present with standardized and prosaic procedures of operation. In a *professional bureaucracy*, skill rather than performance of routine tasks was present. With a *divisional form* of organization, parallel units and/or departments would exist with autonomous managers overseeing the various units. Finally, in an *adhocracy*, project teams might prevail, which addressed specific projects or issues. In regard to HSOs, the principal structure is the machine bureaucracy. However, depending upon the service delivery system present, various amounts of the professional bureaucracy and the divisional form may be evident.

Systems can be simplistically viewed as a package of things which function together in some form of harmony or disharmony. One can also conceptualize a system as being composed of several events which function as a "turn-key" process. As such, there is input, processing, output, and feedback at several stages of the process. The degree to which any system functions smoothly is based upon the process, equipment, and the people managing it.

Cascio (1982) noted that a system was composed of various subsystems, all of which were part of a supersystem. As such, the modern organization was said to be an open system with ongoing interaction of several dynamic environments, internal and external, which provided needed feedback to the process. Landy (1985) suggested that a system was based upon a variety of human engineering factors which usually included some form of communication among the various components. These notions are most relevant to HSOs in the 1980s and beyond.

Without a dynamic environment which solicits, accepts, and processes input from various sources, the organization is doomed to failure as a viable system.

In a machine, various sensing devices serve to monitor the workings of that machine. Siegel and Lane (1982) noted that a system was a broad designation which related to a package of "events, materials, hardware, operations, and processes" (p. 191). Controls are needed to regulate input and output as well as feedback.

A bureaucracy can be compared to a machine in that the operating procedures are usually well defined and incorporate numerous internal and external controls. In terms of past political machines, such as the Huey Long regime in Louisiana, the Mayor Daly machine in Chicago, or the Jimmy Hoffa machine of organized labor, great efforts were made to insure they were well-oiled. Numerous lieutenants were available to ensure that the politico-economic messages were sent forth. If the people failed to comply, they were eliminated in some way or another. Weber (1947) suggested that bureaucracies were composed of various official functions which were composed of rules. As such, rules eliminated the need to decide on each event as it occurred. Activities were standardized. Each member of a bureaucracy was said to be competent in a narrow realm and people functioned through a prescribed hierarchy. A modern bureaucracy may thrive upon rules, confusion, ambiguity, and conservatism. Favell, Favell, Riddle, and Risley (1984) noted that bureaucracies tended to be resistant to change and that long-term control of problems (that is, strategic planning) was not too common. Brunsson (1985) concurred.

Another note on bureaucratic issues. In early 1987, tons of garbage from the New York City area were loaded on a barge and sent out to sea. The alleged issue was centered around no one's wanting to assume responsibility for its disposal. After weeks, and some 6,000 miles of travel around the Atlantic coastal area, the barge once again returned to the New York harbor area. The Associated Press reported that the debris barge docked in Brooklyn, New York, on August 26, 1987. The garbage was to be incinerated, with the ashes being taken to Islip, New York, to rest. Needless to say, no sane organization would waste tens of thousands of dollars on such a farce. A classic example of "that's not my job."

TRADITIONALISM, PATRONAGE, AND TENURE

Webber (1979) noted that *traditional* organizations were characterized by top-down management and that decisions were more often subjective than objective. In regard to human service facilities, Favell et al. (1984) believed that these organizations were often based on bureaucratic tradition, fads, and personalities which tended to defy logic. Other forms of bureaucracies (Webber, 1979) included the *rational* and *contemporary* models.

In the rational model, a pyramid structure of organizational span of control is present. Objectives and goals are better defined than in the traditional bureaucracy. Impersonality and objectivity are frequently present. People tend to be equalized: the strong are moderated, the weak made stronger, as they are lost in the critical mass of the system. With the contemporary bureaucracy, two pyramids are present. A smaller one, composed of managers and professionals, is on top with the worker mass on the bottom. The Horatio Alger myth of working one's way to the top (except perhaps for the Rockefellers, Henry Ford, Ray Kroc, Steven Jobs, Akio Morito, Dave Packard, Lee Iacocca and a few hundred others) is rarely realized by the person with average ability and motivation. The college degree is a key (but not a guarantee) to the upper pyramid or inner circle for most individuals in the ordinary organization. Internal dynasties prevail and a title may not guarantee acceptance. There are instances where a direct-service worker has, through considerable experience and additional education, become a middle manager or gone on to obtain an advanced degree and enter a profession. In such cases, the direct-service worker ethic may persist without acculturation as a professional.

Change is extremely difficult for any form of bureaucracy. Conservatism is a major force. Brunsson (1985) noted that change could be risky for individuals in a bureaucratic system. Efficiency, flexibility, and change were not always present. Avoiding change tended to be more rewarding than initiating it. The internal structure of the organization was self-serving and intrinsic. External forces often conflicted with the status quo and internal subsystems conflicted with one another. Mintzberg (1979) noted that when an organization was under a condition of uncertainty or external pressure, then management might waive the democratic process and act more authoritatively. Additionally, Mintzberg (1981) noted that structure was needed in order to coordinate a variety of work processes. The need for twenty-four-hour residential coverage may require some of Mintzberg's machine bureaucracy (standardization of work and a stable environment).

Many bureaucratic institutions are terminally constipated with vested interests, sacred cows, political pressures, and other omnipotent traditions which serve to perpetuate a form of incest within the system. A form of cannibalism can occur among opposing departments, work groups, units, and other subsystems. Favell et al. (1984) suggested that one solution to our outdated institutions was to burn them down and start over! There may be a touch of merit in this notion.

Packard (1974) said that organizations must not become too rigid. Otherwise, work effectiveness and communication would suffer. This author has observed a number of human service systems in which one would bump into "force fields" when approaching the various department turfs. We have seen this phenomenon consistently in academe. Toffler (1970) felt that most bureaucratic systems were not designed to manage rapid change—and that when they did encounter excessive change, conflicting situations often resulted. In the prevailing unit system at many HSOs, especially the PRFs, the bureaucratic ethic may not advocate change. Thompson (1976) suggested that "production units" did not always cooperate or interface with "innovation units."

The turfism issue can be psychodynamically related to the defense mechanism of *perceptual defense*, a denial and ego-protective device. Here one *protects the clan* against outside invaders who purport to threaten the status quo of the in-group. By erecting barriers to outsiders, one prevents true inspection and evaluation of the internal process. It also promotes a form of pseudo-omnipotence. At the institutional level, one department or service often resists or challenges another department or service. All tend to be somewhat skeptical of the motives of the central office, the feds, or a professional or administrative newcomer. There are dues to be paid. In a decentralized unit system, former department heads or other generalists are not always assimilated into the network.

On the other hand, while the foregoing picture may appear rather bleak, it is obviously not always the case. Any number of facilities subscribe to an energetic and creative spirit which does not condone internal negativism, dysfunctional politics, and petty obstructionism. One issue which seems to facilitate a proactive and non-neurotic organizational style is that of the facility having a for-profit orientation. Of course, this eliminates most of the state-run HSOs. Where there is a profit motive involved, non-productive employees are frequently terminated, new ways of solving problems (and saving money) are sought, and the spirit of competition encourages better quality services. Before I am classified as a heretic or troublemaker, I must add that probably 10 to 15 percent of the nation's state-supported HSOs have a good structure, style, and organizational climate.

Patronage is another issue, though not as direct as it was in the period prior to 1970. For a definition, it is considered here to be the appointment of an individual to a bureaucratic job on some non-merit basis. The same applies to internal transfers. However, with the advent of state merit systems, obvious patronage is not legal. On the other hand, a form of new-wave patronage is occurring in our institutions. This seems to be especially prevalent in our state institutions for the mentally retarded, nursing care facilities, and similar institutions that are experiencing critical staff shortages due to increasing federal standards for staffing of intermediate care facilities (ICFs).

This new patronage is based upon the supply and demand phenomenon of recruiting an adequate labor pool. In particular, direct-care-worker positions are most affected. Characteristically, these jobs are low-paid with few perks. It is not uncommon to process scores of new applicants with minimal screening, testing, or background checks. The patronage of the "favorite son or daughter" has changed to the practice of "any warm body will do." This even occurs in the recruiting of professional staff. There is also an ongoing problem of recruiting qualified professional employees to work in institutions which are located in rural areas. Services and staffing ratios must be met. Some states are even funding college students' professional education in exchange for one or more years of servitude back to the state. Physicians and some other professionals and managers are receiving incentive pay in unclassified positions. I have observed physicians being paid between $35,000 and $70,000 for similar job responsibilities at the same facility. The concept of incentive pay has been occurring in academe for some time. These issues will be addressed further in later chapters.

Also relevant among institutions of the 1980s and beyond is that of tenure. For purposes here, I define tenure as at least ten years of service with a given institution. While one does not usually think of tenure outside of the academic setting, it is very prevalent in our institutions. The greatest prevalence can probably be found in institutions located in rural settings. There are various reasons for institutional tenure. Some include status (best job in town), job security, inability to find a job elsewhere, lack of interest in exploring new horizons, vesting in a retirement plan, and community roots. Some management employees may continue their tenure due to their having a local following as well as being a power figure in the institution. Dynasties are very ego-enhancing. Also, the larger one's realm of power and/or following, the less one may have to be accountable for his or her actions—at least until something adverse happens and organizational heads roll.

The number of tenured employees is generally small in proportion to total employees. However, these employees generally have at least two bases for their power. The first is through an informal network of colleagues; the second can be through a position of power in the institution. In some cases, both are present. Less frequently, a dominant personality may be the source of power. Some may be considered untouchable by others due to social or political factors. The power may or may not be competent power. With professional or administrative employees it may seem that "as goes John or Mary Doe, so goes the institution (or department)." Direct-care employees also have their local, subgroup power base which may or may not involve the intimidation of new workers. New or otherwise less powerful staff are often cautioned about going against these power figures. Yes, business and industry also has these structures. However, in the institutions power does not always follow competence and these people are much more difficult to terminate than in the private sector. Such people can facilitate change, or they can either passively or directly resist change. Innovators and those who actively seek efficiency, progress, and increased productivity can be significantly blocked by such individuals.

MICRO-GOVERNMENTAL ISSUES

HSOs in the public sector are plagued with micro-governmental issues. The lowest level may be the department structure or a professional discipline at a facility with the highest being at the State Central Office level. Traditionally, local facility departments have ruled in their discipline with interdepartmental conflicts often occurring. Some of these problems still exist; however, Teams, Units, Service Areas, and related structures have, in current practice, replaced many of the traditional models in a number of facilities.

Separate institutions or community-based facilities are generally subservient to various levels of state agencies, departments, commissions, and others. We find conflicting issues internally within a facility, between those competing with or being compared with one another, and among various state-level agencies manipulating financial affairs of the local facility like pawns on a chessboard. Politico-economic strategies are intense. McNamara (1986) noted that central offices often became "mini-governments" within a state system.

Downs (1968) postulated a "law of interorganizational conflict," which referred to the notion that almost every group or organization was in some form of conflict with another one. This concept may vary from setting to setting. We have all seen state-level games being played during an election year. Superintendents and other agency heads are frequently serving at the pleasure of the central office or local community board. Central office commissioners and other agency heads are often appointed at the pleasure of the prevailing partisan political system, the governor, or local constituency. Depending on who's in power and the composition of the state legislature, budget appropriations for mental health, mental retardation, correction, nursing-home, and other facilities are often rooted in partisanism. Vested interests tend to be epidemic and lobbying activist groups thrive.

EXTERNAL REGULATIONS, CERTIFICATION, AND SYSTEMS

No HSO can operate without the presence of various federal and state regulations and certification. In order to receive third-party reimbursements, a facility must be licensed and/or certified. Likewise, various professional, technical, and direct-care employees must be licensed or certified. This also affects the ability to recruit employees. Not only do we have the traditional physician and nurse licensure but such technical titles as Licensed Mental Health Technician, Certified Substance Abuse Counselor, Licensed Psychologist and others are, more than ever before, requiring some form of state-based certification or licensure as a condition of employment.

While licensure, registration, or certification does not necessarily guarantee competence, dedication, motivation, potential productivity, or altruism, it does indicate that these individuals have at least been exposed to higher levels of education and/or supervised experiences. Licensure or certification of a facility does not guarantee its compliance with federal or state standards. It merely communicates the standard and then provides a mechanism by which compliance or decertification can be enforced. More on these issues in the chapters on training and recruiting.

MANAGEMENT BY PLAN OR CRISIS?

Management involves the functions of planning, organizing, and controlling, among others. One of the basic lessons of a business or organization is that if it is not managed properly, then the business will fail. Points made by Siropolis (1982) on how to become a successful entrepreneur included the fact that about 90 percent of all new business failures were due to poor management. This included managerial incompetence, lack of management experience, and lack of experience in the product or service area. You may be thinking, "So what!" Well, it is not unusual in HSOs for supervisors, department heads and others to be promoted to their positions for reasons other than management expertise.

In business, people are promoted for reasons of sales or service productivity, public relations skills, communications skills, the ability to align oneself with an upward-moving mentor, being in the right place at the right time, being noticed by an upper-level manager, socializing with the right people, and perhaps a little dumb luck. In human service facilities (especially the state institutions), supervisory appointments are frequently due to a sudden vacancy, an organizational restructuring, seniority, and the "pick of the internal litter." Professionals are rarely trained (and some are significantly incompetent) in the art of management or supervision to the degree that a person is groomed in the private sector (Hinkle and Burns, 1978; Sluyter, 1976). Thaw and Cuvo (1986) especially noted this phenomenon. Some of these people are exposed to the required supervisory training classes and sent on their way. The 5 or 10 percent of the good supervisors and managers rapidly advance to positions of more responsibility (or take better jobs elsewhere).

Most HSOs participate in annual, biennial, five-year, and other planning cycles. If for no other reason, certain external funding sources and/or public expectances require this. On the other hand, many of the public facilities fail to carry out these plans realistically. Some of the reasons are bureaucratic barriers, employee attitudes, and other forces beyond the facility's control. Management is often by crisis, under the shadow of a filed-away long-range plan. Characteristically, the facility will continue to maintain (or cannibalize) itself with or without the plan. The patients must be served, and most employees continue to do their thing.

In the private sector, long-range planning is critical for survival since the competition is also doing it. You either deliver a better product or service, or do it cheaper or faster, or your business fails to survive. On the other hand, public facilities such as general hospitals, nursing homes, halfway houses, private residential treatment centers, some outpatient clinics, and private clinics must be run like a business. (We must take a momentary exception to this in commemoration of Lee Iacocca and his seminal coup of the Chrysler bail-out.) State-run agencies are run like a business, if the way to run a business is similar to the method by which the federal government is run. Captive facilities always have a bail-out provision. You don't close them down when the cash flow is short. The state government merely appropriates more funds until the end of the fiscal year. If the superintendent, director, or administrator is found to be incompetent, the controlling forces merely remove the thorn and appoint someone else, and the process recycles.

It is not uncommon for some HSOs to be managed by crisis within some predetermined semblance of strategic planning. Similar to the person who lacks self-control with credit cards, the dysfunctional facility charges onward, trying this and trying that in hopes of eventually reaching its goals. Favell et al. (1984) noted that PRFs often rush to be all things to all people with employees failing to cope and clients not benefiting. From an international perspective, Virgo (1984) stressed that health care facilities must think critically about the past, present, and future. Structured plans were viewed as both flexible and adaptable to environmental changes while at the same time being positively related to making good decisions in the present.

General hospitals were said to function in five environments: economic, social, technological, political, and legal (Virgo, 1984). PRFs often function more in the political and legal realm than in the other realms. The excellent managers are obligated to make decisions in an uncertain and dynamic environment as well as getting things done through a variety of people with minimal formal control. Peters and Waterman (1982) would definitely concur.

SERVICE AND BUDGET CONFLICTS

Budget allocations have never been adequate to provide optimal active treatment in the PRFs. In the old days, you treated the patients with the available funds and didn't worry too much about it. But the patients helped work in the institution to supplement staff ratios. Cuvo and Thaw (1986) noted that PRFs serving the mentally retarded had such inadequate budgets that the poor staff-to-client ratios made effective habilitation nearly impossible. State legislatures tend to fund bottom-line dollar amounts and generic services. An institution may have an eight-to-one employee ratio but may need a four-to-one ratio for proper active treatment models. Additional budget allocations are often refused by the legislature; however, decertification issues may prompt additional fund releases. Internal politics of an organization may affect whose service or department obtains funding, without regard to theoretical or actual need.

Part of the program-funding problems are in all probability due to a continuing level of conservativism among the general public and the state legislatures and inadequate understanding of the real costs of direct-care services. Throughout history HSOs, especially PRFs, have been poorly funded because society has apparently not wanted to spend too much money for these less fortunate people.

Within a facility, interdepartmental conflicts occur which may result in misguided internal distribution of funds as the result of internal politics. Certain tenured managers may have more leverage in obtaining funds for their programs than do lower-status managers. Some facility administrators may be either indifferent to or opposed to seeking external grant funds for programs. One facility I visited a number of years back had a full-time grantsperson who obtained several million dollars in grants annually. Of several facilities I have visited since 1975, only a few seemed to be interested in, much less seeking, external grant funds. This seems to be especially true for those PRFs that do not promote a research orientation (or in those state legislatures which do not want extra strings attached to their funding sources). Admittedly, the United States presidents since Lyndon Johnson's administration have not been very free with funds for human service programs. The Reagan administration has also minimized the need for federal appropriations in the area of human services. However, there are numerous private funding sources which could be tapped by a facility philosophy which advocated grant-seeking.

SYSTEM ALTERNATIVES

The first alternative which comes to mind is to fund and manage our nation's public sector HSOs like private businesses. While human service advocates have not exactly viewed human services as a business enterprise over the years, some are beginning to do so. This is especially true with the community-based facilities such as halfway houses, outpatient clinics, specialized residential treatment centers, general hospitals with psychiatric units, and others.

Human services is a business. Granted, you cannot always identify, measure, or count an end product as one can count foreign-made American automobiles or fast-food cheeseburgers, but there are outcome measures. Our society is more than ever demanding excellence in product and service. The companies which deliver an inferior product or service do not survive. Peters and Waterman (1982) noted that American companies were held back by their staffs, structures, and systems.

General hospitals, especially the teaching and research hospitals, usually manage to have a flow of funds to promote quality treatment and research. They have fund drives, sell bonds, have various benefactors and patron saints, collect Medicare and Medicaid and other third-party insurance reimbursements, plus have patient co-payments and collection services for those who fail to settle their bills. Even some of the larger retirement homes and nursing care facilities which have apartments and cottages charge thousands of dollars to buy into the system while at the same time charging monthly maintenance fees and rent.

Part of the HSO crisis is due to historic perspective of charity for the mentally ill, mentally retarded, and physically infirm. To institutionalize a person has been in many cases, to absolve oneself of financial and moral responsibility. The institutions would take over in exchange for the person's retirement or social security check. Some even charge a little extra from the family when they can afford it. It is not uncommon for the per-patient cost to reach $30,000 to $60,000 per year in corrections, mental retardation, and psychiatric facilities, with intensive nursing care facilities costing over $20,000 yearly. On the other hand, studies have indicated that community-based residential treatment facilities serving patients with poor adaptive behavior are not much more economical. At the lower end of the budget would be ICF nursing homes, rehabilitation agencies, community detoxification units (other than those in general hospitals and similar non-critical care facilities). When one considers the salary for twenty-four-hour private-duty care and related medical expenses, these costs may not be too outrageous.

The federal government seems to be increasingly shifting the costs of human services to the states. At the same time, regulations are continually being added which restrict a facility's ability to provide services as well as driving up the costs of service delivery. If this is to be the trend, perhaps we need to look at a state sales tax or mill levy to subsidize our facilities. Or, perhaps we could sell some of our obsolete treatment buildings and convert them to low-cost community housing or to minimum security or prerelease correctional facilities. Another option we might consider would to put coin boxes at the fast-food restaurants for donations. What about a community, county, or state donation drive for the purpose of "buying" an extra employee, computer, or wheelchair? We need to begin to be more creative in our approaches to facility funding and operation. One rather cost-effective approach is that used by Governor Mike Hayden of Kansas. He instituted a policy of having prison inmates assist in the work of renovating obsolete public buildings to provide for more corrections space. Other governors are undoubtedly doing the same. On the other hand, one must not forget the infamous statement of former Colorado Governor Dick Lamb, who suggested that the aged had a duty to die (would have allegedly solved some of the PRF crisis).

There are no easy alternatives to traditional service delivery systems or to the bureaucracy. Perhaps the most obvious is to attempt to streamline facility philosophy and operations and to strive to fund and manage them like a private business. In the next chapter I will address the issues of cost-benefit in more detail in terms of some lessons we might be able to learn from private-sector business and industry. But the field of human services is people-intensive; you cannot replace employees with robots (even though you and I both know one or two employees who could be replaced by a robot). Some general system alternatives would include being more cost-effective in operations, rethinking the use of our inefficient and obsolete buildings, obtaining more qualified employees, and increasing the productivity of our existing employees.

3

ORGANIZATIONAL DYNAMICS AND CULTURE

Every organization, small or large, has a unique set of dynamics, culture, and personality. Part is due to the nature of its business, and part is the result of management philosophy which recruits individuals which have a good "fit" to its system. There is a traditional discrepancy between the private-sector profit motive and the public-sector altruistic philosophy. A position is taken in this book that any HSO is functioning as a *going concern* with the goal of helping others in perpetuity; in this sense, it is a business enterprise.

The discipline which addresses the dynamics and culture of organizations is industrial and organizational psychology, a blend of applied psychology, sociology, personnel psychology, and economic psychology. As a separate field, it had early beginnings in 1913 with Hugo Munsterberg. World War I provided a significant impetus to this growing field—United States Army personnel needed some tests to screen inductees. Improved efficiency of mass production (begun around the Ford Motor Company era in the early 1900s) became synonymous with criteria for worker efficiency. The growing interest in fitting jobs to workers led some of the early experimental psychologists to study adverse work environments such as noise and heat and their effect upon fatigue and boredom and thence job performance. Elton Mayo began the Hawthorne studies at Western Electric in 1927, continuing until 1939. These studies investigated various human factors and their interaction with the work environment (McCormick and Ilgen, 1985; Roethlisberger and Dickson, 1939; Siegel and Lane, 1982).

There are essentially two types of business structures in reality: a traditional form, and an entrepreneurial form. In the traditional form, organizational culture is handed down through tradition in the company. Sacred values and cultures are perpetuated as newcomers are indoctrinated to them. The second form, an entrepreneurial business, is on the cutting edge of philosophy and technology. Innovation, change, and a free form are present. Two examples: The Ford Motor Company, and the Apple Computer corporation. In the early years at Ford, there was apparently a conservative model in the areas of corporate climate, values, and marketing strategy, as evidenced by manufacturing only black Fords. The consumer was so elated to obtain an automobile at an affordable price that the black Ford was acceptable at the time. By contrast, Stephen Jobs, the founder of Apple Computer, was (and perhaps still is) a maverick who had a new vision in a new era and would not allow himself to be controlled by a corporate structure. Resultantly, Apple Computer has been a very dynamic and progressive organization, and Steven Jobs has left for bigger and better conquests. Interestingly, according to the June 10, 1987, issue of the *Chronicle of Higher Education*, it was noted that Steven owned about $83 million in Apple stock at the ripe old age of thirty!

The bureaucratic traditions of HSOs have been of the early Ford Motor Company form. The organizational climates have been passed down through generations of governmental conservatism and policy. A *minority* of HSOs throughout the United States could be considered entrepreneurial in policy and function. In particular, the PRFs have not changed much in the past fifty years in terms of their culture. The outpatient clinics, general hospitals with psychiatric units, and specialty proprietary residential facilities and clinics have been more of the entrepreneurial type. In these latter facilities, new treatment techniques and organizational concepts have been in operation for a number of years. Many of the state PRFs are still operating in pre-twentieth-century buildings, have rigid employee chains of command, and become very upset when a radical employee suggests too-rapid change.

PUBLIC- AND PRIVATE-SECTOR PHILOSOPHY

Essentially, the public-sector HSOs believe that there is a service to society to be provided and tax dollars are expended. Consumable and capital expenditures usually defy logic. At times, purchases are made from the lowest bidder, and not necessarily from the firm which offers the best product. This can result in problems and inefficiency for employees. Only in the last few years have HSOs come under significant scrutiny from federal funding sources to become more accountable for services delivered. Funds are requested; funds must be expended. If a facility fails to spend the entire fiscal-year budget allocation, it often loses that amount of funding the next fiscal year. It is a concept of "if you didn't spend it, you didn't need it in the first place." Thus, an HSO may make last-minute purchases at the close of the fiscal year in order to expend all allocated funds. Funds must be spent in order to be justified. The tail wags the dog.

By contrast, a private-sector enterprise must cut costs and constantly improve efficiency if the market competition is to be met. There are ongoing decisions of whether to make, buy, or lease. Production-cost issues are foremost. Quality control, customer satisfaction, and profit margins are crucial. If the business is to remain a going concern, it must continue to meet the competition in the marketplace, gain increasing segments of the market share, and strive to cut costs of products and services in order to deliver a competitive product or service to the customer. One of Steven Jobs' philosophies is that a computer should be created from a vision of what *could be* rather than building upon what *is*. Such insight can well be applied to HSOs. On the other hand, the HSOs which are not state-run frequently subscribe to the private-sector philosophy. General hospitals are competing with other general hospitals to have the best cardiac unit, oncology unit, or emergency medical unit. Some are beginning to cut costs to the patient by providing alternative ways to provide service.

While public- and private-sector enterprises share a concern for the customer or patient, their inherent philosophies are often at odds. In the private sector, human productivity is crucial if the competition for products and services is to be met. With the public-sector enterprises, especially the PRFs, maintaining the status quo is often more important than increasing employee productivity or being on the cutting edge of human-services technology.

The significance of how important an organizational climate is, is that organizations, public and private, frequently select an employee who is believed to "fit"—one who can be expected to subscribe to the organizational culture. The best-qualified applicant is not always hired. Team players are wanted. If you are not a team player, forget about working for McDonald's, Hewlett-Packard, or IBM. The image is crucial. The organizational climate is akin to the cultural mores of a society. Subcultures, in-groups, and other structures prevail, but all contribute to the unique personality of a given organization.

While the team spirit is crucial for the employee to have if the individual is to survive, Iacocca (1984) noted that most important decisions were made by individuals, not committees. Knowledge was shared in committees, but when committees replaced individuals, productivity was noted to decline. Iacocca suggested that "in order to hit the duck, you have to move the gun." Committees are not famous for being able to act quickly and to facilitate a decision.

The best companies subscribe to a philosophy of productivity through people. Management and employee interface is crucial. Too often at PRFs and other HSOs management remains distant and is more concerned with meeting compliances, and providing shift coverage than they are in motivating and supporting their employees. They are so busy "shooting alligators" they forget their main objective was clearing the swamp. I will exclude the better HSOs for the most part here. Iacocca (1984) noted that Japanese cars were good, and that such performance began with the workers who were more productive than their United States counterparts. The attitude of the Japanese worker is "How can I help?" rather than "That's not my job." In Japanese companies, the employee wears many hats—a professional may pick up a broom and sweep the floor if needed.

One factor that will serve to demoralize and inhibit employee productivity is the absence of feedback. The feedback process may be informal, such as daily progress reports, or formal, such as the organizational performance appraisal. Too often supervisors and managers fail to reinforce good performance of their employees. Feedback is frequently lacking. The average supervisor or manager is usually too busy with his or her own problems to worry about the supervisees. Some actively avoid giving performance feedback, due to either a lack of concern or wanting not to be bothered with details.

A number of years back I briefly worked for a major chain store as a salesperson—a very regimented experience. Praise and reinforcement were essentially lacking. Periodically, the supervisors would show the sales staff an "error report" which pointed out cash register inaccuracies. Once a month the store manager would use the fifteen-minute coffee break, the employees' own time, to pass out scarce bits of praise for the prior month's sales. Peters and Waterman (1982) indicated that part of the dominant culture in a number of large companies was to punish an employee for an error. Now I am not saying that an employee must have continual praise in order for his or her job to be done. I am saying that praise and other constructive feedback when due will significantly improve performance. Peters and Waterman (1982) noted that in the excellent companies, the systems were designed to produce winners—and that when one excelled, the winning was celebrated. Non-monetary incentives were frequent, and a lot of hoopla occurred.

ORGANIZATIONAL CLIMATE AND PERSONALITY

HSOs are often overburdened with countless rules and procedures. This communicates that employees are not entrusted to make independent decisions, and it communicates that unless there are some rules, chaos among employees will occur. Webber (1979) noted that when policies and procedures were followed blindly, direction was lost, and the organization was in danger when spontaneity disappeared. Peters and Waterman (1982) also suggested that the excellent companies insisted on top quality, listened to their employees, and treated them as adults. On the Japanese front, the chairman of Sony Corporation, Akio Morita, noted that American managers were not very concerned about their workers.

In both HSOs and private enterprise, the employee needs to feel some control over his or her destiny. When the organization is overextended with countless rules and policies, the employee may very well feel a victim of the system, and this will serve to institutionalize the person. Two-way feedback is crucial.

According to Peters and Waterman (1982), managers at Hewlett-Packard used a style of "management by wandering around," while United Airlines used the concept of "visible management." Communications were emphasized. At many HSOs, supervisors and managers are too often found in their offices or otherwise out of reach of their employees. The employee often feels that management does not know what is going on and that "if my supervisor had to work my shift, well...." We all need someone we can trust and can talk to when a personal or work crisis occurs. First-hand knowledge of what your employees are doing is critical and two-way dialog is even more important. Supervisors and managers must be accessible and treat their employees decently.

The worst companies and a number of PRFs are similar in their organizational climate and their interactions with employees. It is paradoxical that although HSOs are in business to be facilitative and helping to the patients, many supervisors and managers are poorly trained in the methods of helping their employees to increase their productivity, job satisfaction, and morale. The best companies and a smaller percentage of PRFs, as well as a large percentage of the better private-sector HSOs, utilize a management style that encourages two-way communication and emphasizes the notion of productivity through people.

As Peters and Waterman (1982) noted, "The excellent companies are marked by very strong cultures, so strong that you either buy into their norms or get out" (p. 77). The public HSOs are not quite as rigid in this respect. On the other hand, the privately operated HSOs are more oriented toward private-sector philosophy and require strong ac-culturation by their employees. Favell et al. (1984) stressed that PRFs often rushed to be all things to all people, with employees not coping and patients receiving minimal benefit. Ideas and employees were re-cycled without first conducting cost-benefit studies; quick fixes were done. Brunsson (1985) believed that organizational efficiency in HSOs did not always correlate positively with an attitude of flexibility, and that this inflexibility could thwart change. Peters and Waterman (1982) supported these ideas in that they said the top companies ac-tively strived to ward off calcification by experimenting more and per-mitting small failures as part of the process.

In the overall area of organizational climate and proactive corporate personality, several companies have been heralded as being on the cutting edge of employee technology. These include: Digital Equip-ment, Hewlett-Packard, IBM, Schlumberger, Texas Instruments, Data General, Intel, Raychem, Wang Labs, Eastman Kodak, Johnson & Johnson, Procter & Gamble, Bristol-Myers, Avon, Levi Strauss, Merck, Revlon, Caterpillar Tractor, Dana Corporation, 3-M, Delta Airlines, Marriott, McDonald's, Disney Productions, K-Mart, Wal-Mart, Dow Chemical, Du Pont, and Amoco. These and others not mentioned met the criteria for excellent performance in organizational attitude toward employees and customers (Peters and Waterman, 1982).

What distinguishes these companies from those who are mediocre? Among other things, it is an excellent organizational climate and per-sonality which places significant emphasis upon the employee as a viable, important, and significant contributor to the goals and success of the organization. Another excellent company, Frito-Lay, "achieves its objectives through people." IBM has an excellent human resources program which includes performance planning, counseling, evaluation, merit pay, open communication, and an extensive company educational program. At Hewlett-Packard, the "H-P Way" stresses a focus upon people, an excellent working environment, employee freedom to be innovative and creative, and the absence of time clocks (Harris, 1985; Peters and Waterman, 1982).

At Frito-Lay, a large portion of its success has been built upon the philosophy that the highest goals can only be achieved by developing and maintaining a loyal and efficient work force which gains satisfaction from their work (Brunsson, 1985). Dana Corporation is an old timer—since 1904. Prior to about 1980, Dana was a product-oriented company; since then it has become market-oriented. As one of the better companies, its philosophy is to keep the employees informed about the organization, its profits, and other items. A broad-scope monthly newsletter is distributed, as well as a letter from the chairman to each employee every three months. One-on-one communication is emphasized. Another part of Dana's climate revolution was to place its three volumes of policies and procedures in the "round file." They reduced their three volumes to one page—no corporate procedures at Dana. Autonomy and entrepreneurship are also encouraged, as well as minimal supervision. Dana developed a list called "Forty Thoughts," including the following notions: people are the most important asset, one should promote from within, people respond to recognition, entrepreneurship should be encouraged, simplify things, communicate fully, discourage conformity, break organizational barriers, and insist on high ethical standards (Cowie, 1985).

Delta Airlines has a climate which resembles the Japanese philosophy—strong culture and actively helping one another at work. Delta was said not to have a layoff policy and subscribed to an open-door philosophy (Rollins, 1985). William G. Ouchi, author of *Theory Z* (1981), later postulated the M-Form (or multidivisional) organization. In this structure, the operating units are semiautonomous. Each unit has its own product line while drawing upon the corporate service area resources. Such an organization is between the centralized and the decentralized. If the M-Form structure works well, the employees work as a team. There must be a balance between competition and teamwork if this structure is to work (Ouchi, 1985). To a great extent, our PRFs are involved in some of the M-Form structure with their unit systems and some eroding of traditional departmental structures.

In essence, then, the excellent companies subscribe to a philosophy of productivity through people, few rules and policies, flexibility, entrepreneurship, open-door policies, teamwork, a strong organizational culture, and employee autonomy. On the negative side, Kets de Vries and Miller (1984) described some organizational climates of neurotic organizations. Five dysfunctional climates and three cultures were noted.

The *paranoid* organization emphasized controls. Outside threats were identified, strong internal budgetary controls were present, executives withheld information, and the climate was cold, rational, and hypersensitive. Reality was distorted, and employees lost capacity for spontaneity due to defensive attitudes. The *compulsive* organization was obsessed with perfectionism and triviality, was not spontaneous, was tense, dogmatic, and had an internal locus of control. Indecisiveness, postponement, and near-sightedness were common. With the *depressive* structure, an external locus of control was present which incorporated a fatalistic orientation and an impoverishment of pleasure-experiencing within the company. *Schizoid* companies were noted to be detached, flat, lacked the capacity for praise or criticism, had a lack of interest, kept at a distance to others, and might display aggressiveness. Organizations with a *dramatic* flair were noted to engage in self-dramatization, sensation-seeking, exploitation, superficiality, and subjectivity; their employees would feel used or abused.

Along with their five organizational typologies, three cultures were observed. The *fight/flight* mode was oriented to defensive or escaping practices. The world was viewed as either good or bad, with inside or outside enemies to be dealt with. The *dependency* culture assumed that others must be nourished and protected. The leader was idolized. Finally, the *utopian* culture was somewhat future- and fantasy-oriented. Subjectivity, long-term planning, a deliberative style, goals without means, and democratic processes were noted. The authors noted that with the pathological organization, one or two key executives often set the tone for the company.

The dysfunctional organizational styles mentioned above can be found in any number of traditional companies as well as with some public-sector HSOs. Flexibility and innovation are often absent and employees may feel victimized by the system—which leads to burnout, lowered productivity, and poor morale. If I may be so bold, some of our PRFs could fall under the classifications of paranoid, compulsive, and schizoid. Such personality structures may very well be the result of decades of bureaucratic traditionalism which has maintained itself partially due to the fact that society has placed our PRFs in the roles of societal outcasts. Another cause may relate to significant numbers of long-tenured employees who, for whatever reasons, guard their departments and services strongly.

FACILITY AND EMPLOYEE COST-BENEFIT

The concept of *Utility* as postulated by Cascio (1982) and other organizational authorities deals essentially with the area of cost-benefit in personnel selection, or the assessment of socio-economical factors of organizational programs (Katzell and Guzzo, 1983). It is a conceptual and statistical process by which decision-makers are able to consider costs, consequences, and anticipated payoffs among various alternatives. It has been used successfully in cost-benefit analyzing of training programs and staffing, and in determining the extent to which an employee's level of productivity is estimated to be cost-effective (Landy, Farr, and Jacobs, 1982; Schmidt, Hunter, McKenzie, and Muldrow, 1979; Schmidt, Hunter, and Pearlman, 1982; Weekely, Blake, O'Connor, and Peters, 1985). More succinctly put, Utility theory involves the use of cost accounting procedures by which to attach a dollar value to proficiency and productivity (Landy, 1985). Additionally, Utility frequently incorporates the use of valid and reliable personnel selection tests by which to measure potential employee productivity. An additional technique, *Meta-Analysis* (Glass, McGaw, and Smith, 1981), has been gaining in popularity as an additional method by which to analyze the large body of research which has accumulated on studies of Utility (Hunter and Schmidt, 1983).

Inherent in the bureaucratic functioning of a PRF is an adherence to tradition and conservatism. Similarly, building facilities, programs, and employees often lack optimal cost-benefit. Our old buildings are very inefficient in regard to energy management, maintenance, and programming. Organizational attitudes may not actively seek a more rational or cost-effective way of doing things. On the other hand, policies of austerity may not provide for adequate funds by which to provide optimal and innovative treatment for patients. Employees have job security but few of the material, and at times emotional, perks of the private sector. While PRFs purport to operate on a cost-per-unit philosophy (the processing of the greatest number of patients at the lowest cost), it has been noted (Allen, Heatherington, and Lah, 1986) that the absence of a competitive philosophy has impaired efficiency in the systems.

Addressing international issues in health care, Wood (1984) presented the *Clinical Care Unit* (CCU) concept whereby a given procedure (in general hospitals) was given a point and dollar value in terms of diagnosis, surgical procedure, and the patient's "point-in-progress toward recovery." As such, each unit of value identifies the relative difficulty and amount of staff time for a given task or procedure. This is a significant step toward the application of utility theory in HSO operations.

Some of the more progressive HSOs do provide more perks to their employees. This is especially true for those HSOs which are proprietary, except perhaps our nursing homes, and minor treatment centers. The general hospitals and private hospitals and clinics frequently have benefits and physical facilities that approach the quality of these in the private sector. A limited number of the public mental retardation and psychiatric institutions are modern and approach the structure and climate of the better private-sector companies.

Our PRF physical facilities are often of nineteenth-century construction. Numerous vacant structures are present on the grounds, which are slowly eroding as the result of deinstitutionalization. State governments seem to have a lack of concern for these buildings and seldom incorporate long-range planning for their renovation and use. Our communities in which PRFs reside have needs for low-cost public housing, halfway houses, and minimum security correctional facilities, but we continue to build new buildings while our old structures are not renovated.

Utilization of employees is not always cost-effective. Some employees are burned out, unmotivated, and unchallenged. Others are merely putting in time until retirement. Still others are highly motivated and productive. Due to internal political structures, various PRFs may not utilize their employees to best advantage. Organizational restructuring may occur, but without optimal employee utilization. An unproductive employee or one with a perpetual obstructionist attitude is never terminated, just reassigned. The state merit systems will not allow termination without due cause, such as a major violation of policy or a crime. Facility departments and services, regardless of their HSO category, may promote employees to supervisory and management positions in accordance with civil service rules of seniority and then purport to train these individuals in the basics of supervision and management. One department will have a critical need for secretarial assistance while another has extra secretaries. Due to issues of turfism and internal power structures, the secretaries may not be assigned based on need. Some are idle while others are overworked.

Needed supplies and equipment may not be purchased, due to budgetary constraints. As a result, both employees and programs suffer.

Computer software that is needed may go unpurchased because it does not carry an approved budgetary line-item designation. Needed program development may not occur because new employees cannot be hired until the next fiscal year. Four tradespeople may be on a work assignment to install one door—a carpenter, a locksmith, a painter, and a supervisor. In the private sector, one handyman would do all of this. On the other hand, the maintenance department is understaffed and cannot cut the weeds on the grounds or fill a pothole in the driveway. We can thank our unions for making jobs so specific that our tradespeople will not cross occupational barriers and do what needs to be done. I doubt if William Ouchi or Akio Morito (much less Dana, IBM, or H-P) would allow such inefficiency in one of their companies.

At one facility a new computer system was installed for the purpose of program tracking. Big bucks were spent in setting up the system. Due to some state-level roadblocks, the system was put on hold. At last count, the system was mothballed. At another facility, one professional employee assisted another department in setting up a data system. Following large expenditures of time, the individuals who wanted the system failed to follow through in project completion—other priorities arose. (Needless to say, the same happens in the private sector.) Several professionals at another facility developed a rather good system for tracking patient behaviors which was to be used on a facility-wide basis. During a departmental reorganization and staff transfers, the system was scratched and thousands of dollars in staff time were wasted.

Employee turnover is another area in which HSOs are not very cost-effective. However, the problem is not easy to solve. For most of the employees, the work is unglamorous and poorly paid, and the benefits are not the greatest. Add to this the prevailing organizational climate at many facilities, and one has a mechanism by which turnover is predictable. This turnover is similar to that in the retailing, restaurant, and similar non-professional job markets. There is not often an organizational camaraderie among workers except perhaps with direct care groups. Employees work to have money to enjoy life while at the same time realizing their professional ambitions. Part of this is due to the difficult working situation in human services and its lack of inherent glamour. Few of these facilities have an organizational spirit which would be evidenced in employee clubs, organizations, or HSO-sponsored get-togethers and outings. If we would incorporate just a touch of Theory Z into our HSOs, we just might improve our efficiency as well as team spirit and co-worker cooperation.

I am not sure if HSOs, especially those publicly funded, will ever be truly cost-effective and inculcate an organizational climate which approaches that of the excellent companies. Too much tradition and conservatism. But some are definitely moving in that direction. As more supervisors, managers, professionals, and administrators become aware of the more proactive climate, there will undoubtedly be improvements in the HSOs. It takes a lot less energy for employees to be nice, cooperative, proactive, and team-oriented than it does for them to think of ways in which to make others' jobs more difficult and to continue protecting their own turfs at all costs.

4

MOTIVATION: THE PRODUCTIVITY ANTECEDENT

A business enterprise, whether in the private or public sector, is generally concerned about motivation and concomitant productivity among its employees. An employee who is neither motivated nor productive is an expendable item of excess baggage to the business. Essentially, most individuals are motivated, for whatever reason, to survive in some way or another. The degree to which some survive better than others is based upon a complex formula of individual desires, needs, tensions, strivings, aspirations, and other phenomena. A morbidly obese person may have a food obsession; a morbidly thin, anorexic person probably has a pathological aversion toward being fat. Some employees are motivated simply to pay their bills and maintain the status quo. Others may be motivated to become the highest-paid individual in the company, to have the greatest number of cars sold, or to have the greatest number of patients who successfully recovered.

HISTORICAL NOTIONS OF MOTIVATION

In *"Passions Of The Soul,"* René Descartes (1649) expressed his belief that there was a dichotomy of mind and matter. Human behavior was said to be rational, while animals had instinctual drives. Much later, McDougall (1908) emphasized the area of instincts as did Sigmund Freud around the turn of the twentieth century. Freud believed that humans only had two motivations, work and love. As a result, his theories suggested, we do not always have conscious control over our behaviors. In order to address the issue of innate behaviors, Woodworth (1918) was convinced that another motive might be present. The term *drive* was created. A drive was considered to be the overall activity process of humans or non-humans.

The position that humans and non-humans might have some *purposive* function was emphasized by Tolman (1932). Lewin (1938, 1951) developed his theories of motivation around human behavior rather than that of non-humans. In essence, Lewin postulated that humans had both psychological and physiological needs which created a state of tension and resulted in the individual seeking to reduce that tension through action. Around the end of the Great Depression in the United States, Murray (1938) postulated twenty specific needs which humans attempt to satisfy.

Murray's needs were: abasement, achievement, affiliation, aggression, autonomy, counteraction, defendance, deference, dominance, exhibition, harmavoidance, "infavoidance," nurturance, order, play, rejection, sentience, sex, succorance, and understanding. The reader is referred to Murray for full explanation of these needs. An outgrowth of his need theory was his Thematic Apperception Test (TAT). Prior to about 1960, the concepts of drive (need), reinforcement, and incentive dominated the majority of the literature on motivation. Hull (1952) addressed the concept of *habit strength*, which was essentially a function of the intensity, frequency, and latency of accumulated reinforcements the individual had received in the past in regard to a specific response. E. L. Thorndike's Law of Effect was the primary basis for Hull's theories. This law postulated, in essence, that individuals tended to repeat those behaviors which were perceived to be satisfying or reinforcing; or, that rewards tended to increase behavior while punishment served to decrease behavior (Hilgard and Bower, 1966). Hull's motivational component was designated as *drive* which involved a general stimulus or force toward activity.

In general, motivation theory which related to organizational behavior was described by Campbell and Pritchard (1983) as being either process- or content-based. The process theories included those of Hull (1952), Lewin (1938, 1951), Skinner (1953), Tolman (1932), Vroom (1964), Adams (1965), Festinger (1957), Porter and Lawler (1968), and others. On the other hand, the content theories were related to the area of *need* and included those of Murray (1938), Maslow (1954), Alderfer (1969, 1972), Herzberg (1959), and others. Additional models included Adams' (1965) Equity Theory, Expectancy Theory (Locke, 1968), and the Need Achievement theories of McClelland (1951, 1961), McClelland, Atkinson, Clark, and Lowell (1953), and Atkinson (1964, 1965). Some Attributional theories such as those of Heider (1958), Jones and Davis (1965), and Rotter (1966) have been described.

THE MOTIVATION TO WORK

Significant *content* theories to be discussed further include those of Murray, Maslow, Herzberg, and Alderfer. *Process* theories to be addressed will be those of Tolman, Skinner, Festinger, Georgopolous et al., Vroom, and Porter and Lawler. Other theories which were based on these two processes, in part, include those of McClelland, Atkinson, Rotter, Adams, Locke, and Ryan.

The Content Theories

Traditionally, content (need) theorists have suggested that an individual was inherently motivated toward homeostasis due to the presence of a tension state from opposing systems being out of balance: when one had a pain in the stomach which suggested hunger, then food was sought.

As previously noted, Murray's (1938) theory involved twenty needs. Maslow (1954) suggested there was a hierarchy of five human needs (physiological, safety, belongingness and love, esteem, and self-actualization). In this model, lower-level needs had to be satisfied before the individual was ready to strive for and fulfill higher-order needs. This theory has failed to be consistently and empirically validated based on current research on motivation and productivity. And, as Landy (1985) noted, Maslow's theory probably had more historical than pragmatic value. His genesis was rooted in area of instinctual drives (a carry-over from the Freudian era) in that "Man is a wanting animal and rarely reaches a state of complete satisfaction except for a short time. . . . It is a characteristic of the human being throughout his whole life that he is practically always desiring something" (p. 69). There is a certain amount of appeal in Maslow's work even if his Hierarchy of Needs theory has been weak from a scientific standpoint.

Herzberg (1966) proposed that individuals had two sets of needs, *motivator* and *hygiene*. The hygiene needs were of a maintenance nature and included such items as pay, security, co-workers, general working conditions, and company policies. In this respect, Smith, Kendall, and Hulin (1969) developed the Job Descriptive Index (JDI) which addressed Herzberg's hygiene-need area. Motivator needs were at a higher, intrinsic level and were considered to be growth needs. Motivator needs might include challenges, stimulation, and autonomy.

Here, individuals might desire such perks as independent and/or responsible work, accomplishment, and altruism. *Job enrichment*, according to Herzbergian theory, was one way in which an employee could be progressed from hygiene- to motivator-need levels. In general, the need theories which included those of Maslow, McClelland, and Herzberg have not stood up to significant empirical tests. Herzberg's was perhaps a little more plausible and pragmatic in that, unlike Maslow's, a hierarchy of satisfaction was not required. On the other hand, it is difficult to conceptualize that any employee who is having problems paying the rent would be very concerned about higher-order satisfactions.

Alderfer (1969, 1972) postulated three basic needs in his ERG theory of motivation: *existence*, *relatedness*, and *growth*. These were based upon Maslow's hierarchy paradigm. In effect, the existence needs were of a survival nature, a gain-versus-loss struggle among people. Food, money, and safety were in this category. In the area of relatedness needs, Alderfer stressed affiliative processes, a sharing of cognitive experiences with others. Open sharing of information was part of this relatedness. Third, one's growth needs were of a higher-order structure, similar to those of Maslow's self-actualization components. Alderfer did indicate, however, that if a need was not satisfied, then it might become even more urgent.

In sum, the content (or need) theories of Murray, Maslow, Herzberg, and Alderfer were based more or less on some form of need continuum or categorization. Murray postulated twenty needs, Maslow had five, Herzberg had two categories, and Alderfer presented three. For the most part, need theories have not been empirically substantiated in content-validational and cross-validational studies. They all have a certain degree of intuitive appeal, and some components may be valid in some situations.

The Process Theories

A few historical concepts were presented earlier. The works of Descartes, McDougall, Woodworth, Levin, and Hull were the beginnings of modern theory. These cognitive theories generally addressed various intellectual and personality constructs as opposed to the instinctual theory of Freud and others. For our purposes here, the work of Tolman,

Skinner, Festinger, Vroom, and Porter and Lawler will be discussed next.

Purposive Behavior. Edward C. Tolman, as did other early process theorists, based most of his notions upon the area of experimental psychology. On the other hand, the content theorists did most of their work in the area of differential psychology. The area of industrial and organizational psychology borrows from both realms. Tolman's *Purposive Behavior in Animals and Men* (1932), held a behavioristic view and significantly rejected the introspection model (such as Freud's). Behavior was *molar* (an act of behavior that had distinctive properties of its own), goal-directed, incorporated environmental issues such as path-goal, pursued the *principle of least effort*, and behavior was teachable. As Hilgard and Bower (1966) noted, Tolman held the position that performance was regulated by rewards and punishments.

Operant Conditioning. B. F. Skinner had roots in behaviorism and the experimental setting, using rats and pigeons for his subjects. His *operant conditioning* concepts were first presented about 1930 with a series of papers on the subject. Skinner (1953) believed there were two types of behavior, *respondent* and *operant*. When a behavioral response was due to known stimuli, it was respondent; when responses could not be linked to a given stimulus, then they were designated as operants. Skinner (1938) noted that when an operant was followed by the presentation of a reinforcer, then the strength of the operant was increased. This notion can be compared with Thorndike's law of effect mentioned earlier. In estimating Skinner's position on motivation, Hilgard and Bower (1966) noted that reward increased operant strength whereas punishment did not have a corresponding weakening effect.

Cognitive Dissonance. Festinger's (1957) theory of *cognitive dissonance* is another process-theory model. In an oversimplified form, the cognitive dissonance paradigm suggests that the individual will experience a tension state when discrepant cognitions are present. Resultantly, the individual will seek to eliminate these discrepancies in order to reduce the tension state. For example, when two individuals are in disagreement over an issue or concept, then discrepant cognitions tend to occur. These discrepancies become dissonant and unresolved discrepancies create tension and conflict among the parties concerned.

Instrumentality Theory. Several theorists have been involved in the area of *instrumentality*. In essence, this model addresses a "What's in it for me?" concept. The first model of instrumentality which related to the work environment was presented by Georgopolous, Mahoney, and Jones (1957) and was called *path-goal* theory. Thus, if an employee perceived that hard work would lead to attainment of more personal goals, then the employee would probably produce more.

One of the more popularized models of instrumentality theory was the VIE theory of Vroom (1964). VIE, or Valence-Instrumentality-Expectancy, may be relevant for the issues among HSOs. *Valence* is designated as the attractiveness or non-attractiveness of a given object in one's work environment. Money or recognition might have a positive valence, while low pay and working as a direct care aide might have a negative valence. With the *instrumentality* portion, the relative outcome (what's in it for me?) is considered in regard to expected effort. The *expectancy* component is an if/then probability statement: "If I expend a given amount of effort, then will the payoff be commensurate?"

Porter and Lawler (1968) presented another version of instrumentality theory. The *Porter-Lawler Model* rejected the traditional concept of need theory. Nine components of their theory were postulated. First, they suggested that the *value of reward* was relative to the individual and that different people attach different valences to perceived outcomes. Second, *perceived effort-reward probability* was the practical component that effort should equal reward. Third, *effort* was noted to have both an energy expenditure and a performance component. Increased effort did not necessarily improve performance. Fourth, *abilities and traits* were said to be unique to the individual and usually set the upper limits of performance. Fifth, *role perceptions* included the individual's perception of what constituted successful performance on a given job. This was related to the self-fulfilling prophecy or Pygmalion effect. Sixth, *performance* referred to the overall level of the individual's accomplishments on the job. Seventh, *rewards* included both intrinsic and extrinsic reward areas. Eighth, *perceived equitable rewards* related to whether or not the individual perceived that the reward received was really fair. Last and ninth, *satisfaction* was termed by Porter and Lawler as a "derivative variable." In this respect, it was a comparison between what the employee felt was an equitable reward and the one which was actually received.

Other Relevant Paradigms

Need Achievement. McClelland (1951, 1953) suggested that certain cues or stimuli in the environment had motivational properties which were based upon the individual's successes or failures in the past. This theory incorporated a quantitative theory of those things which the individual perceived to be pleasant or unpleasant. Any positive increase of stimulation over the existing state would be perceived to be pleasureable, with a negative deviation being perceived as unpleasant. Atkinson (1957, 1964) further addressed McClelland's theories of need achievement. Accordingly, achievement-oriented behavior was due to a conflict between approach and avoidance behaviors. Every possibility for success had its opposite option for failure. As a basis for some of our current theories on motivation, Atkinson suggested that achievement was based upon three areas: motivation to succeed, the probability that success can be achieved, and the incentive value upon success. This incentive was also considered to be "pride in accomplishment."

Locus of Control. Internal versus external locus of control might also be a factor in an individual's motivational strivings. Rotter (1966) postulated that when an individual believed that he/she was in control of his/her own behavior and destiny (internal locus of control), then achievement would probably be more rewarding. An external locus of control presented a situation in which the individual believed that success is due to fate or the control of others.

The ultimate belief in externally caused events was included in the concept of *Learned Helplessness* (Seligman, 1975). In this regard, Seligman noted that "when a man is faced with noxious events that he cannot control, his motivation to respond is drastically undermined" (p. 30). He also noted that when one allowed depressive and helpless feelings to rule one's body, the desire to live might be reduced.

To digress briefly, Ewing (1967) noted that extreme helplessness could also facilitate death. For example, cockroaches were reported to have definite dominance hierarchies (social pecking orders). A subordinate cockroach would lower its antennae when it approached a dominant cockroach. This posture often led to the attacker halting its offensive move. When repeatedly aggressed by dominant cockroaches, the subordinate one would die.

Equity Theory. This theory assumed a concept of balance and homeostasis in motivation. As a "balance theory," it borrowed from Festinger's (1957) concepts of cognitive dissonance. In an oversimplified form, the cognitive dissonance paradigm suggests that the individual would experience a tension state when discrepant cognitions were present. Resultantly, the individual would seek to eliminate these discrepancies in order to reduce the tension state.

Another theory of work motivation based upon balance theory was Adams' (1965) version. In this model, the individual formed a ratio of inputs in a given situation to expected outcomes in the situations. Inputs were those things which the individual contributed; outputs were perceived to be those primary and secondary rewards which the individual received for effort. In effect, if the individual perceived that his or her rewards were equitable with those of peers, then equity would be achieved. For example, when a worker surpassed another worker in productivity, then this condition created cognitive dissonance for the other workers. In order to reduce this tension, other workers might either meet the higher production or encourage the faster worker slow down to return to the norm of productivity.

Instrumentality Theory. Instrumentality theory as presented by Georgopolous et al. (1957) was called *path-goal* theory. Current concepts of instrumentality as developed by Ryan (1970) and Locke (1968, 1970) are more operational and relevant to HSOs. Locke pointed out that harder goals elicited higher performance and that those individuals who consistently set high goals were high performers. When one considers the effect of difficult goals on performance, Locke's theory indicated that difficult goals produced high performance; with instrumentality theory, such as Vroom's, the reverse appeared to be indicated.

Ryan (1970) noted that human behavior appeared to continue until a goal was reached and that one might become frustrated when behavior was interrupted during the course of goal-attainment. Finally, with need-achievement theory, goals with intermediate levels of difficulty seemed to encourage high performance.

RELEVANCE FOR THE WORK ENVIRONMENT

Motivation theories abound. Additionally, about every management consulting firm will have its own prescription for employee motivation and its implications for productivity improvement. There does not appear to be any panacea theory for a private- or public-sector company or organization. Pure theories generally work best for their originators. For most purposes we generally need to extract the most relevant parts of one or more theories and use them in a pragmatic manner. In terms of process or content theory bases, the pure content theories, such as Murray, Maslow, and Herzberg, do not appear to have much practicality. On the other hand, some of the process theories such as those of Skinner, Tolman, Vroom, Adams, Festinger, Porter and Lawler, as well as those of Locke, McClelland, Atkinson, and others may have some utility.

Since about 1900 motivation theory has come a considerable distance, with the development of a variety of systematic models. Sigmund Freud believed that people had essentially two motivations: work and love. This was perhaps a touch reductionistic, however.

While Maslow's hierarchy of needs theory has a certain degree of esthetic appeal, it subsumes that one cannot realize the next higher level of need gratification until a lower-level need has been fulfilled. We can observe numerous instances where the theory cannot hold up to empirical test. For example, a person who chooses to be an economic and societal dropout and live in a bug-infested tenement building may prefer to be an eccentric loner while at the same time, perceiving himself or herself to be in a self-actualized utopic state. One might also have strong belongingness and love needs without having any safety needs. Maslow's need hierarchy theory does not indicate a course of action for the manager.

Herzberg's two-factor theory simply suggests, in part, that to motivate people you enrich their environment—but enrichment of jobs has backfired in some work settings. Herzberg's two-factor theory, like Maslow's hierarchy of needs theory, has not stood up well to empirical analysis. While Herzberg made a significant contribution to motivation and satisfaction theory, his concept of two unipolar continua (motivator versus hygiene factors) cannot be defended, logically or empirically.

Achievement motivation theorists previously discussed, such as Murray, Atkinson, McClelland, and others, had somewhat more plausible positions. Both individual and environmental considerations were present which addressed approach and avoidance behaviors to a task. Adding to the continuing issues in motivation were Rotter's concepts of locus of control. Seligman's concept of learned helplessness may very well be significant for the issue of motivation and productivity, in that, if one feels helpless to confront the environment, then withdrawal and lack of motivation may occur.

While the instrumentality theories are better than some others, they are still in the developmental stage. There are some indications that they may have some empirical support. Managers can relate to instrumentality in that it can be understood and the principles can be applied. Instrumentality or path-goal theories have a little more credibility from a empirical point, although effort does not always lead to reward. Vroom's VIE theory, however, appears to have more relevance for HSOs. Porter and Lawler had another version of instrumentality which may also be relevant.

Goal-setting theorists, such as Ryan and Locke, incorporate the concept of feedback into the process. And, as many authorities have observed, feedback is crucial for the proper functioning of any system or its components. But goal-setting approaches may not work very well with line-level employees. It is primarily suited for use with managerial and professional employees. In a similar vein, Drucker's (1954) management by objectives (MBO) has not been of universal benefit across organizational settings.

With goal-setting theory, feedback is crucial. Matsui, Okada, and Inoshita (1983) found that the effectiveness of feedback varied with the individual. Poorer performers produced more with feedback. Additionally, Locke, Shaw, Saari, and Latham (1981) found minimal support in the literature for employee participation in goal-setting as a motivator. The presence of goals seemed to be more important than employee involvement, per se.

Adams' and others' approaches to equity theory may have more impact in current times due to the continuing relevance of equal opportunity in employment, especially equity in pay. As a type of balance theory, one expects reward to be commensurate with effort, as in VIE theory. However, equity is not always evident among HSO structures. Work situations which are perceived by others to be lacking in equity may result in such strategies as work slowdowns, threats of quitting, or actual product or service sabotage. In order to create (or restore) equity for some employees, non-tangible benefits may be given. These may be such perks as a title, a better office, more freedom, or flexitime. As Landy (1985) suggested, the concept of fairness or equity was contingent upon the worker's perceptions that outputs (rewards) were proportional to inputs (efforts). State merit systems which conduct annual job surveys are working toward equity—seeking balance among occupational class salaries and benefits across state geographical boundaries as well as equity with salaries for comparable classes in the private sector.

The principles of operant learning theory are practiced in a form called applied behavioral analysis (behavior modification). An Antecedent-Behavior-Consequence paradigm is inherent. For example, a paycheck every two weeks (or monthly) is fixed-interval reinforcement. Failure to come to work results in punishment (probably being fired). Operant learning principles (Skinner, 1953, 1974) are the basis for modifying behavior. Other important basic references are Bandura

(1969), Ferster and Skinner (1957), Kazdin (1984), Skinner (1969), and Tosi and Hamner (1974). In more recent years these principles have come under the concept of *organizational behavior management* (OBM). OBM has also been called organizational behavior modification, and OB-Mod. The concepts of OBM will be discussed in a later chapter.

Operant learning theory has been used by various private- and public-sector organizations for a number of years, purposively or inadvertently. In reality, most organizations (public and private) use some form of OBM since it is traditionally easier to use than such hygiene factors of Herzberg as "job enrichment" or other nebulous paradigms. Organizations are composed of people, and people are generally human. Humans have grown up under a reward-punishment model since as children they may have been spanked for misbehaving or given ice cream for helping mother or father.

Operant learning theory has a wide variety of applications and probably is the most accepted and used in the real world. We can externally motivate employees (temporarily) by such simple philosophies as "work or get fired," or we can strive to relate a system to our unique company or organizational structure.

However, current practice in some excellent companies indicates that productivity and employee commitment can be enhanced through team-building, one item noted in Peters and Waterman (1982). This is not always the case, of course. Different jobs and different company climates will determine the efficacy of such procedures. The simplest form of goal-setting is with the "things to do today" list. We all know that without some systematic play or work our behavior can become random and lack significant direction. Pragmatically, goals need to be set. Whether or not goal-setting theory will evolve as a predominant approach remains to be seen.

Brunsson (1985) indicated that the degree of risk in a given course of action would influence one's level of motivation toward that action. Peters and Waterman (1982) believed that intrinsic motivation played a larger part than extrinsic in the performance of high achievers. They also suggested that peer pressure, rather than supervisory or management directives, can be a significant motivator.

Brunsson indicated that motivation seemed to influence commitment for the individual, and that the employee must feel that a course of action was worthwhile prior to making a commitment toward a goal. Once commitment has occurred, then the individual is more likely to carry the activity to completion. Feedback was mentioned as being an effective motivator as well as a mechanism for increasing performance

(Reid and Whitman, 1983). Positive feedback was found to be very powerful for both morale and productivity. On the other hand, if it was not used properly, employees might become suspicious of a monitoring and feedback system.

Feshbach and Weiner (1986) noted that *attributions* (positive or negative mental sets about a situation or toward an individual) might influence one's success or failure. In this respect, consider the hoopla surrounding such firms as Mary Kay Cosmetics, Amway, Herbalife, and others. The followers strongly inculcate a notion of ultimate success; this can be observed in their theatrical sales presentations. On the other hand, these flamboyant and highly successful firms do motivate their followers! The self-fullfilling prophecy, or Pygmalion effect, is very interwoven in these examples.

There have been thousands of articles published on the subject of motivation, productivity, morale, commitment, and job satisfaction. Some things we know. First, job satisfaction does not cause higher productivity. Second, an employee can be coerced to produce for a while, but without the employee buying into the system, commitment and productivity will not necessarily continue at a high level. Third, employees who are higher producers seem to be more satisfied in their jobs and seem to have a greater commitment to the task at hand. Fourth, system morale, productivity, job satisfaction, and commitment seem to increase when there is a high level of communication and when the employees perceive that management is supportive of them. For most people, work serves as a major segment of their lives. If work is not meaningful, then family and other areas can suffer. As leisure time is becoming more important for people, work is a means by which one can afford the leisure pursuits. Some employees view the workday as a monotonous routine with the only perks being the socialization among co-workers; these individuals look forward to the end of their shift.

Stanton (1983) suggested that evidence in recent years has indicated that many individuals no longer see the need for hard work and feel entitled to sundry benefits for their efforts. It is the concept of "they owe me." Meyer (1978) indicated that employee costs are increasing, and that productivity and commitment are on the decline. It was further noted that inadequate and constructive feedback, lack of the supervisor's sensitivity to an employee's needs, denial of information, lack of support, and intrusion into the employee's psychological and physical job space could lead to employee de-motivation. As Cavanagh (1984) suggested, as rewards decrease, employee motivation usually drops to minimal levels. External motivation which uses a system of rewards and punishment can backfire on the company, especially when rewards can no longer be given.

In effect then, public sector HSOs will probably incorporate a variety of theoretical orientations into their functioning. Portions of two-factor and instrumentality theory will be used as will be goal-setting. Equity theory incorporates all of those issues which employees perceive as being fair and equitable. From a practical employee management standpoint, most organizations can utilize the principles of operant learning theory to their advantage. In all of these constructs, feedback should be foremost. Too many managers or organizations use OBM or other processes to "manage" employees, without involving the employees in decision-making and without completing the system dynamics by using the feedback loop.

For one to be productive, one must be motivated to attend to task, for whatever intrinsic or extrinsic reason. As will be discussed in the next chapter, job satisfaction is not significantly related in a positive direction to productivity. Thus, one may be highly productive and hate the job if the need is there to remain productive. Baird (1984) studied 250,000 health care employees in 423 hospitals. In essence, employees who perceived that they were challenged, involved, communicated with, cared about, and part of a work team displayed lower absenteeism and turnover along with higher productivity than those employees lacking in these perceptions.

While various theories have suggested a variety of methods by which to address employee motivation and productivity, no one theory offers a panacea. HSOs will need to incorporate those concepts and techniques that best fit their organizational structure, climate, management style, service delivery system, and composition of employees.

5

PRODUCTIVITY IN HUMAN SERVICES

There is a general notion that if a human or non-human is motivated to do something, then some amount of action or productivity will result. But, from a macroeconomic level, productivity may be temporarily declining. Tuttle (1983) noted that between about 1963 and 1983 productivity among all nations declined; the United States and Canada evidenced a negative rate of growth since 1978. The U.S. Bureau of Labor Statistics reported that between 1967 and 1977 the nation's annual rate of productivity growth averaged about 1.5 percent; for the period of 1978 through 1980, the nation's growth rate averaged about -0.33 percent (Bureau, 1985). While national growth rates reflect the macroeconomic picture, organizational issues are at the microeconomic level.

ISSUES IN PRODUCTIVITY

From a pragmatic standpoint, productivity might be perceived as a results-oriented, outcome-measurable phenomenon. *Productivity* was viewed as being related to production units, while *efficiency* incorporated an economic factor into the model. As a systems issue, Coulter (1979) and Balk (1975) indicated that efficiency was related to overall effectiveness. *Effectiveness* (Price, 1977) was the extent to which an organization accomplished its overall goals. For example, a psychiatric hospital, ICF/MR, or correctional facility that successfully releases a large percentage of its clients into the community might be an "effective" facility, all things being equal. However, effectiveness and efficiency may not be co-variant.

According to Tuttle (1983), productivity may be conceptualized as having five processes which can be measured: productivity awareness, analysis, planning, implementation, and evaluation. To increase productivity an HSO must first be aware that productivity is deficient. Analyzing the components of the deficit, planning for improvement, actually implementing the productivity plan, and finally assessing the effects of the improvement strategies are crucial. For example, if a PRF does not incorporate program budgeting concepts into its financial planning, then it is difficult to assess the cost-effectiveness of a given program. Too often reduction of costs and/or productivity improvement is externally imposed by state budget offices, whereas the facility itself might be content with the status quo.

While productivity has been characteristically described as the ratio of output to input, it has been very difficult to measure at the human service level (Fuchs, 1969; Heaton, 1977). It is rather easy to measure both quantity and quality of tire lug wrenches; however, measuring the results of psychotherapy, habilitation, or rehabilitation has not been very easy. Balk (1975) described productivity as: Productivity = Efficiency + Effectiveness. Or, Output/Input + Output/Measurement Standard (for output) = Productivity. Campbell and Pritchard (1983) reiterated the notion that performance had been described as "performance = f (ability × motivation)" (p. 64). And they noted that "performance is not synonymous with the effort, ability, or a combination of the two" (p. 65). The issue of individual choice to perform was noted as a critical issue. In essence, performance is more complicated than mere will to produce, effort, and other factors. Systems issues often affect the overall performance domain.

In the HSO setting, productivity is frequently related to clarity of organizational objectives and goals, clarity of employees' job assignments, the level of stress present, turnover, employee and organizational commitment, and a frequent problem of effecting significant "cures" among patients, clients, residents, or inmates as the case may be. There can also be blockading of productivity efforts as the result of poorly trained employees, misguided internal employee transfers, and organizational restructuring. A viable alternative to measurement of therapeutic success is to address systems efficiency, including internal procedures. It is not uncommon for PRFs to be under purchasing contracts with suppliers in the so-called spirit of free enterprise. When a contract expires, then a competitor may start from scratch. Here are two examples. One PRF had a certain brand of telephone system. When the next fiscal year's contracts were let, the competitor installed a new phone system, including removal and replacement of the facility's phone wiring! Down-time from phone installers disrupting office activities as well as having to train employees in the new system was significant. Another PRF changed contracts for computer systems. Existing microcomputer brands were removed and a competitor's brand was installed complete with some software unfamiliar to the employees. Personnel had to be retrained in the new system and software. Thousands of dollars in productivity loss from staff was evidenced with little improvement in efficiency (if not a setback) for several months.

Shetty and Buehler (1985), in summarizing the components of those private-sector companies which had excellent productivity philosophies, indicated that a company must have widespread commitment among its employees. Productivity, quality, human resources, and a commitment to action were needed. They, as well as Peters and Waterman (1982), believed that the excellent companies incorporated a strong regard for their employees as the key to productivity.

Too often supervisors and managers become so engrossed with shooting alligators on a daily basis that they become remiss in facilitating employee productivity. The excellent companies facilitated productivity and innovation by encouraging a spirit of entrepreneurism among their employees. Traditionally, *entre*preneurism has referred to a mode of self-employment, whereas more currently *intra*preneurism has referred to independent project-based action within the organization. Mechanic (1973) believed that bureaucratic systems tried to standardize the activities of their employees, and, as Thaw, Benjamin, and Cuvo (1986) noted, management might issue directives which removed freedom of choice from the professional—which may serve to reduce productivity. The intrapreneur who seeks significant autonomy in a bureaucratic structure may encounter monumental barriers to his or her efforts.

Productivity effectiveness is two-fold: the *employee's* and the *organization's*. If these two levels do not function in a symbiotic way, then one may work against the other. For example, a productivity-conscious HSO may perform all of the correct human resource tricks but have a habit of hiring below-average employees. On the other hand, quality employees may be recruited, hired, and placed, but the organizational culture and structure may preclude these excellent employees from remaining very long. The previously mentioned concept of utility is significantly involved in personnel selection and placement (Cascio, 1982; Landy, 1985; Landy et al. 1982; McCormick and Ilgen, 1985; Schmidt et al. 1979; Hunter and Schmidt, 1982). While the pioneering work of Taylor and Russell (1939), the Taylor-Russell Model, was a gross measure of selection efficiency, current issues in utility analysis are considerably more precise.

In the last chapter, it was noted that intrinsic or extrinsic motivation (or a combination) may very well precede productivity. On the other hand, an employee can be coerced to produce, though not forever. There is a notion that unless the employee has some driving force to produce, productivity will not occur. This force may be as simple as the fear of being fired, or it may be a higher-order need for recognition, altruism, self-esteem, or serving clients.

If we consider that utility means any monetary improvement over the status quo, then any improvement in productivity would result in a dollar savings. For example, the Bureau of the Census reported that in 1982 there were about 282,000 employees employed in about 525 psychiatric hospitals serving about 151,000 patients, with a budget of about $7 billion (Bureau, 1985). Speculating a median salary of all employees (janitors to psychiatrists) to be about $20,000 per employee, then a total payroll for 282,000 employees would be about $5.6 billion dollars. If, mind you, we could obtain a conservative 5 percent improvement in productivity, we would save about $282 million dollars! Even at a single facility with an annual personnel cost of $15 million, a 5 percent improvement in productivity would be a savings of about $750,000! That amount of savings could erect a small treatment building, fund a fair amount of research, or hire about eighteen licensed Ph.D. psychologists. I am talking about a *twenty-four minutes per day per employee* which is put to better use! I could go into any HSO, especially the PRFs, and in all probability determine at least 10 percent of operations which could have improved efficiency.

I can hear the skeptics now. "Our people are already pushed to the limit, stress is high, and you want to push them 10 percent more?" Not exactly. Here is a valuable tip. Do you have at least one area at your facility where you require records to be kept three different ways? I know of some facilities where the same information is duplicated using four different forms! Only one or two of the forms are required by HCFA or other regulatory agency. Why four forms? Because that's the way they have always done it! Get rid of one duplicate form (with all associated personnel costs—filling out, typing, retyping, putting in folder, reading it, etc.) and you will probably save up to 5 percent of those professional employees' personnel costs. Unlike the general hospitals and other for-profit HSOs, most PRFs are *not* profit centers in the true sense. Some inculcate a modicum of cost-effectiveness in terms of curtailing patient costs per year and providing minimal benefits and perks for their employees, but it doesn't go much further. Such forms of austerity may be self-defeating in the long run.

The biggest productivity "black hole" is in an HSO's handling of paper. It is not always easy to cut some of it out, but with better systems awareness it can be done. At one HSO in which I worked, I routinely spent about 10 percent of my time doing routine clerical things—getting things copied, typing or hand-writing my own memos, entering routine data onto a microcomputer, affixing routing slips to materials sent to other staff. Considering my salary and benefit package, if a secretary had been available to do the work, the difference in personnel costs (between me and a secretary doing the work) would have been an annual savings of about $2,400. Multiply that by ten administrators and you could have hired a minimum of one full-time secretary. Despite my appeals to administration, they failed to be convinced that I needed clerical support. Another "black hole" is continuing to employ two poorly trained and non-productive employees to do a single job. There are scenarios like this throughout the HSO field. Hasenfeld (1983) noted that about 12 percent of all U.S. workers were employed in HSOs, which represented about 27 percent of the GNP. Think what *this* savings would be?

In essence then, the nature of productivity is utilizing people and systems to the best advantage. An improvement in function can thus have the effect of increased productivity. Then, if people are motivated to do even more, the savings can be enormous.

ORGANIZATIONAL DYNAMICS AND PRODUCTIVITY

The chief executive officer (CEO) sets the climate for the organization. This CEO is placed in that position based upon state HSO goals and priorities, and a CEO who fails to carry out the mandates of the central office, governing boards, or other authority is removed.

I am familiar with at least one HSO where the CEO functioned in a rather low-key role. The water was not disturbed and the person was rarely seen by the employees. The central office did not appear to have any problems with this person. The second and third in command were the power forces, and they were very content with traditional structures—this was modeled by a number of tenured employees. The excellent employees did not remain at this facility very long. Conversely, another facility back in the 1960s and 1970s had a second name, "Center for Human Actualization." The CEO was a brilliant, dynamic, and people-oriented administrator. This person *led* the facility on the cutting edge of innovation. Employees were sent to numerous workshops and seminars (in- and out-of-state); there was a full-time grantsperson; several new programs were implemented, including a horticulture unit and a harness racing track. These facilities were at opposite ends of the continuum.

Recalling Weber's (1947) views of a bureaucracy, a modern bureaucracy is somewhat less rigid, but not always. Policies, procedures, and traditions significantly affect the dynamics which in turn affect productivity. Organizations operate within a framework of group boundaries, and these boundaries are subsets of the group structure. As Hackman (1983) noted, behavior in organizations is due partly to individual and partly to organizational constructs, and research on the organizational side has been less prevalent. The organizational structure and climate will have a definite effect upon the motivation and productivity of the individual employee.

Lawler (1983) noted that organizations contained a number of control systems such as budgets, performance evaluations, and other structures. HSOs characteristically have many control systems which may exceed practicality, at times to the point of diminishing returns. As Lawler also indicated, the individual tends to perform in relation to the amount of effort expended. Control systems may very well produce dysfunctional employee behavior. For example, we are all cognizant of HSO departments or units which submit budgets in excess of anticipated expenditures. The reason is that budgets are generally cut prior to funding. The circular planning mode continues.

In regard to organizational structure, Lawler suggested that small organizations were more flexible in providing incentives than were larger ones. Employees generally believed their input and performance had a greater effect upon the organization. In HSOs which have smaller departments or units, there is a tendency for the employees to have more input and potential effect upon the functioning of the organization. Large structures, as in centralized systems, tend to bury the employee in the hugeness of the organization.

MOTIVATION TO PRODUCE

Rotter (1966) believed that individuals function under internal, external or both forms of control. The externally motivated individual (often the support workers) will generally perform under any structure, especially if a job is needed to earn money. On the other hand, those functioning under an internal locus of control (many professionals and managers) will need more facilitative and intrapreneurial structures for their full development.

Organizations which operate under an authoritarian structure will seriously inhibit employee creativity, productivity, and positive morale. Traditional bureaucratic structures have had a wide span of control with little two-way communication. Where the CEO is authoritarian, mandates, edicts, spontaneous policy issuance as a manifestation of paranoia, and other self-defeating behaviors may occur. This climate becomes contagious. Similarly, the supervisor, manager, or administrator who is obsessed with the notion that knowledge is power will purposively withhold information so as to spuriously elevate his or her feelings of omnipotence, or due to a feeling of job insecurity. Employees are kept in the dark about critical information which is only issued under a rigid guideline of "need to know." Employees may feel that it is a hopeless situation (Seligman's learned helplessness, 1975) and that any effort to be creative or innovative will be met with resistance. Motivation to produce seriously suffers.

Other organizations may operate under a facade of affiliation and supportiveness, but in reality they are operated by a core group of "good ole boys" or "good ole gals" who manipulate systems. More on this later. More optimistically, those organizations which advocate and actively promote open, two-way communication, employee involvement in decision-making, and a spontaneous system of concern for one another will enhance motivation. People want to feel they have something worthwhile to contribute to the system.

Recalling some notions of instrumentality theory in motivation (Porter and Lawler, 1968; Vroom, 1964), people have a need to expect reward based upon effort. If one's effort sinks into the quicksand, then motivation would be expected to drop. Similarly, the goal-setting theories of Locke (1968, 1970) and Ryan (1970), suggested that people progressed toward a goal until a barrier was encountered which elicited frustration. Because employees may also expect that effort should be rewarded in an equitable fashion (Adams, 1965), organizational climates can either hinder or facilitate motivation.

Humans usually have a desire to have knowledge of what is happening to them, and want to have some input into their destinies. A facilitative organizational system can greatly enhance fulfillment of these needs. When employees are "done to," then frustration and anger can result. In the case of PRF which experienced significant scrutiny by HCFA during an inspection of their programs, all levels of employees experienced emotions which ranged from indifference to significant stress reactions. They felt helpless, out of control, and morale was low. An effective CEO mobilized the employees toward positive action and thwarted continued negative feelings among employees.

Management philosophy has made significant strides since the work of McGregor (1960) who postulated the *Theory X* and *Theory Y* styles of management. Theory X essentially postulated that people were inefficient, lazy, would probably steal you blind, et cetera. Managers of this style often tended to be authoritarian and/or paranoid. Theory Y suggested that people had higher-order needs and were essentially "good." With Y-style managers, affiliative and democratic climates were frequently present. While there may be some truth in this reductionistic philosophy, practice has generally disproved the efficacy of this bipolar structure (as has been done with Herzberg's two-factor theory of motivation). For the most part, we can say that HSOs strive to treat their employees as worthwhile human beings; however, this is not always the case.

In effect, some form of intrinsic or extrinsic motivation appears to be prerequisite to any level of productivity. Employees can be briefly coerced to produce; however, the organizational climate will seriously suffer if this model is pursued. While every administrator hopes for productive as well as contented employees, the two do not necessarily go hand in hand. The issues of job satisfaction, morale, and commitment are important facets for a positive organizational climate—but the system will probably continue with or without these higher-order phenomena.

JOB SATISFACTION

The identification and measurement of job satisfaction is difficult at best. Theorists and researchers alike continue to disagree as to just exactly what job satisfaction is. Issues in satisfaction have been discussed in the literature for nearly 100 years, but we have yet to develop a highly valid and reliable measure of this elusive construct. A brief chronological history of relevant job satisfaction issues seems in order.

Frederick W. Taylor's theories of "scientific management" incorporated the notion that economic incentives were important in satisfaction in the early twentieth century (Taylor, 1911). However, current thought has failed to consistently relate satisfaction to monetary rewards. Later, Munsterberg (1913) made the observation that not all workers were dissatisfied with monotonous, repetitive tasks. This holds true today. Monotony and repetition is a relative thing—the Golden Arch of the McDonald's chain is an excellent example. The relationships of job satisfaction to factors such as age, marital status, education, and religion were studied by Fryer (1926) where no significant relationships were found among a sample of male applicants for commercial jobs.

Hoppock (1935), during about the same era that Elton Mayo was conducting the Hawthorne studies, produced the first comprehensive effort on the topic of job satisfaction. In some rather classic studies, he observed that there were more satisfied workers than previously thought. For example, about two-thirds of all workers surveyed in New Hope, Pennsylvania, reported they were satisfied with their jobs. Furthermore, among a group of teachers who perceived themselves to be highly satisfied with their jobs, Hoppock noted that these individuals seemed to have better mental health, better human relationships, and that older teachers reported more job satisfaction. These teachers also believed themselves to be more successful. Job satisfaction was noted to be related to educational status. Finally, Hoppock suggested that the construct of job satisfaction could be measured reliably.

A pioneer in the study of the relationship of need satisfaction to job satisfaction, Schaffer (1953) suggested that the amount of dissatisfaction which occurred was determined by the strength of the individual's needs or drives. Additionally, it was noted that satisfaction was related to the extent to which the individual could perceive and use opportunities to satisfy needs. Also related to need theory, Roe (1956) stressed the role of occupational choice in the satisfaction of individual needs as related to Maslow's (1954) theory of human motivation. Roe strongly believed that employment was interfaced throughout all of Maslow's need hierarchy, from physiological safety to self-actualization. Vollmer and Kinney (1955) investigated job satisfaction and educational level. They noted that persons with high ability levels might be more dissatisfied with their jobs if they were not allowed to apply their total talents to the work setting. In that case, selecting the best qualified person for a job might not be the best choice, since the person's expectations might be too high and therefore would lead to dissatisfaction.

Recalling Vroom's (1964) theory of work motivation which was adapted from Lewin (1951), Vroom proposed that satisfaction was the product of valence (value to the individual) of outcomes (such as high social status) and the perceived instrumentality (effectiveness) of the job in producing those outcomes. It was predicted that a worker would be satisfied if the expected effectiveness of the job in producing a highly valued outcome was realized. In the spirit of this VIE theory, Katzell (1964) regarded job *dis*satisfaction as the result of the discrepancy between the amount of a stimulus experienced and how that stimulus was valued. Value, according to Katzell, was the magnitude of a stimulus which evoked the most pleasurable effect. Dawis, Loftquist, and Weiss (1968) indicated that satisfaction represented the worker's appraisal of the extent to which the work environment fulfilled his or her requirements. This notion was related to Vroom's VIE theory and Adams' equity theory.

From a broader standpoint, Seybolt (1976) investigated the general hypothesis that relationships between characteristics of the work environment and the level of employee satisfaction were moderated by employee education level. Three constructs of job satisfaction were studied: pay, job variety, and task complexity. Among a sample of 926 public sector workers in municipal and county positions, the Job Descriptive Index (Smith, Kendall, and Hulin, 1969), was administered. Results indicated that the employee's level of formal education moderated the relationship between work environment characteristics and job satisfaction. Additionally, job and work organization per se were crucial to job satisfaction among more highly educated subjects. For most interactions, chi-square values were significant at < 0.02 level. This level of significance was less than optimal for a firm interaction.

Job satisfaction among about 4,700 full-time workers in the United States was studied between about 1972 and 1978 (Weaver, 1980). A single question was asked: "On the whole, how satisfied are you with the work you do—would you say that you are very satisfied, moderately satisfied, a little dissatisfied, or very dissatisfied?" The majority of the subjects reported that they were very satisfied with their jobs.

Loftquist and Dawis (1969) perceived job satisfaction to be a function of the "correspondence between the reinforcer system of the work environment and the individual's needs, provided that individual's abilities correspond with the ability requirements of the work environment." As such, job satisfaction was said to represent the employee's appraisal of the degree to which his or her work setting fulfilled the requirements of the individual. Again, another reference to VIE and/or equity theory.

Organizational factors, such as inequities in promotional and salary increases, could be a primary source of worker discontent (Porter and Steers, 1973). Here, the early theories of Taylor (1911) seem to be revisited. The issue of worker age and tenure was also examined by Hunt and Saul (1975). They failed to find a positive relationship between job satisfaction and age for female workers; however, there was a U-shaped curve for male workers. In this respect, new male employees and long-tenured employees were reported to be more satisfied, and employees with medium length of tenure employees the least satisfied. Hunt and Saul also noted that one's level of job performance, age, and length of tenure with an organization's reward system could be contributing variables in these relationships.

Finally, in an extensive survey of about 5,000 U.S. households, Linden (1984) reported that nearly four out of five Americans reported they were satisfied with their jobs. About one-third reported being very satisfied. This supports the early work of Hoppock (1935). Linden also noted that job satisfaction seemed to improve with age, with the sixty-five-year-old and over group reporting the greatest level of satisfaction. Among those under age thirty-five, about 22 percent reported being very satisfied. The degree of satisfaction seemed to increase with income. Little difference among respondents' perceptions of their job satisfaction was observed when analyzed by the nine geographic regions of the United States. Linden concluded that about 24.9 percent were very satisfied, about 53.9 percent were satisfied, about 14.5 percent reported being dissatisfied, and the remaining 6.6 percent indicated they were very dissatisfied with their jobs.

A recent analysis of the issue of employee dispositional (personality trait) factors in relation to job satisfaction was done by Gerhart (1987). An analysis of data from about 12,680 young men and women derived from a cohort of National Longitudinal Surveys of Labor Market Experience was done. Results suggested that changes in situational factors (e.g., job complexity) may have an effect on global job satisfaction. It was suggested that well-designed personnel programs might help increase job satisfaction.

In summary, job satisfaction has been purposively studied since about the turn of the twentieth century with the work of Taylor (1911). Hoppock (1935) conducted the first extensive, systematic study of job satisfaction. Need, VIE, and equity theories seem to have relevance for analysis of job satisfaction variables. Since about 1935 there seems to be a consistent pattern that about two-thirds to four-fifths of the workers in the United States as a whole seem to be satisfied with their jobs. Males and females do not necessarily report satisfaction similarly; younger and older workers, those in higher status positions, and those with higher incomes appear to be more satisfied.

From a systems standpoint, Thorne and Thaw (1986) noted that when employees had expectations for an open and decentralized structure in the workplace and these expectations were not met, then cognitive dissonance could demoralize the employees. Unresolved, this dissonance was also said to contribute to mistrust of the system itself. Thaw and Wolfe (1986) suggested that employee morale could be affected among direct-care workers when satisfaction was not present. High absenteeism, being critical of the system and others, and resistance might be coping strategies. Buffum and Konick (1982) indicated that job satisfaction research in mental health organizations had been a neglected topic. They observed that the more satisfied employees worked in a decentralized (unit) system, had professional job titles, were over the age of forty-five, had about average educational level, and had been employed at the facility either less than four or more than ten years. These findings seemed to be similar to those of previous studies. Job satisfaction seemed to improve when client functioning improved.

Among employees at PRFs serving the mentally retarded, Sarata (1975) suggested that an absence of client progress might be a source of technician job dissatisfaction. Zaharia and Baumeister (1978) investigated job satisfaction among 500 employees in three PRFs. Generally, technicians (aides) had lower job satisfaction scores than those reported by industrial workers.

A new index of job satisfaction, the Job Satisfaction Survey (JSS) (Sluyter, Mukherjee, and Hinkle, 1985) was used by Sluyter and Mukherjee (1986) to examine job satisfaction constructs which were based upon Herzberg's (1959) notions of motivation. This twenty-four-item questionnaire addressed twelve hygiene and motivator factors of Herzberg. Each was measured on a pair of questions using a seven-point Likert scale. This questionnaire was also compared with the Job Descriptive Index (JDI) of Smith et al. (1969) and the Kunin Faces Scale (Dunham and Smith, 1979). Among 357 surveys distributed, 201 (56 percent) were returned. About 36 percent of the men and about 64 percent of the women responded; respondents' mean age was about thirty-six years, mean tenure was about five years. Results suggested that the twelve Herzbergian factors were related to the five factors of the JDI, and satisfaction was negatively related to burnout and factors on the Faces scale. The authors suggested that the JSS had sufficient concurrent validity with the JDI, based upon canonical correlations, to use this scale in the PRF setting. This writer must be skeptical of the relevance of these findings inasmuch as prior research on the viability of Herzberg's two-factor theory has not stood up well in the applied setting.

In sum, the issue of job satisfaction has produced well over 5,000 articles since the turn of the twentieth century. Hoppock's classic work (1935) has appeared to stand the test of time since a number of these issues hold up today. Job satisfaction does not predict productivity. The majority of workers across the United States appear to be very satisfied with their jobs. More educated, higher paid, younger, and older workers seem to be more satisfied. Low- and higher-tenured workers have reported that they were more satisfied. There is a possibility that middle-aged and middle-tenured workers may be experiencing some form of "middle-age crisis" and indecision, whatever this phenomenon is in reality.

Direct-care (technician or aide) workers do not appear to be as satisfied as their professional and higher-paid counterparts, and they may be less satisfied than lower-level industry workers. Part of this may be due to the high stress and demanding work required of direct-care employees. Satisfaction levels among male and female employees may not be similar.

Finally, there may be some credibility in the notions of equity in terms of perceived effort and expected rewards in regard to one's own satisfaction levels. Job satisfaction seems to be independent of types of organizations and business and industry structures. People tend to be satisfied about the same, across settings, but some variability is noted among the constructs previously noted. Some aspects of satisfaction may be related to the employee's perceptions of his or her commitment to the organization, and the organization's commitment to the employee. These are discussed next.

COMMITMENT AND JOB INVOLVEMENT

Commitment can take two directions: the employee toward the organization, or the organization toward the employee. Unless there is a symbiotic relationship between the two, employees may be at odds with the organization and vice versa. Since about the mid–1970s, the issue of commitment has become a topic of increased discussion. Rabinowitz and Hall (1977) suggested that job involvement (commitment) might be negatively correlated with absenteeism. In regard to organizational process, Zaharia and Baumeister (1978) believed that extreme absenteeism and turnover might be indicators of an maladaptive organizational process. They also noted that *job withdrawal* was a failure of one to participate on the job which could range from an applicant's failing to apply for a job, to such behaviors as being late for work, poor job performance, being absent, and leaving the job.

Porter, Steers, Mowday, and Boulian (1974) perceived commitment to be the degree to which the employee identified with a given organization. An employee's emotional attachment to the goals and values held by an organization was perceived by Buchanan (1974) to be another facet of commitment. O'Reilly and Chatman (1986) suggested that commitment research appeared to lack consensus with regard to the process by which an employee becomes committed. Organ and Hamner (1982) noted that the general finding in the area of job satisfaction and turnover was that the satisfied employee was less likely to terminate, all things being equal, but a chance for more pay could be a definite incentive.

Eisenberger, Huntington, Hutchison, and Sowa (1986), in summarizing some research on commitment, noted that economic factors, such as the employee's believing a job change would not be beneficial, could be important. They also suggested that there might be a social exchange between the employee and the organization which might reinforce commitment. It was further suggested that attributional phenomena, reciprocal behaviors of employee and organization, effort-reward paradigms, and related social exchanges might be involved. Finally, they suggested that "employees form global beliefs concerning the extent to which the organization values their contributions and cares about their well-being" (p. 501).

Commitment has also been termed "job involvement." In this realm, attendance/absenteeism, psychological attachment to the organization, behavioral participation, and job choice have been included (Cheloha and Farr, 1980; Reichers, 1986). Eisenberger et al. (1986) indicated that reviews of a number of studies on organizational commitment had failed to produce much evidence for the relationship between commitment and absenteeism or productivity. Cheloha and Farr found in a study of 159 state government employees that both job satisfaction and job involvement were inversely related to absenteeism, a form of commitment. O'Reilly and Chatman (1986) found an inverse relationship between job identification and turnover.

In the Japanese mode, Ouchi (1981) noted that Japan's industrial productivity had increased about 400 percent since World War II. This can be compared with the United States' and other nations' slight decline in productivity noted earlier (Bureau, 1985; Tuttle, 1983). Ouchi noted that "the nature of things operates so that nothing of consequence occurs as a result of individual effort. Everything important in life happens as the result of teamwork or collective effort" (p. 42). Japanese firms were noted to be supportive, egalitarian, primary groups where people fulfilled their personal and emotional needs in the process of serving the company. While this Theory Z model (a hybrid American-Japanese structure) has not been exactly transferable to American systems, there is some merit to the philosophy. Commitment to the company is supreme; in return, the employee has lifetime employment. In the American setting, a high level of team spirit and commitment can be found in such companies as McDonald's, Mary Kay Cosmetics, Hewlett-Packard, and others. Team players and hoopla are ever-present.

George and Baumeister (1981) examined employee withdrawal and job satisfaction among about thirty-eight house managers and twenty administrative personnel in a randomly selected group of twenty-one mental retardation agencies in Tennessee. It was believed that turnover might be due, in part, to organizational dysfunction. Rotter and Mills (1982) examined the linkages between organizational commitment, intent to remain on the job, and attitudes toward absenteeism among about 368 professionals at two hospitals. Results indicated that the work climate, quality of work life, and relations with the physicians were related to commitment and desire to remain at the hospital. Among those who were prone to absenteeism, burnout appeared to be a significant moderator variable. As such, absenteeism was again found to be independent of turnover.

In the area of conflictual goal orientations in a sample of about 124 mental health professionals and managers, Reichers (1986) observed that perceived conflict levels of these two groups was positively related to commitment. Commitments were believed to develop over time and may be a multidimensional construct.

Additional perspectives on absenteeism and turnover will be discussed in a later chapter. However, some of the issues relating to employee commitment and job involvement appear to be concerned with an inverse relationship between absenteeism and commitment, and in some instances, the presence of a dysfunctional organizational system, climate, or process. There appears to be an indication that commitment can be two-way, employee toward the organization and vice versa. Factors such as economics, psychological attachments, and esprit de corps may also be significant. As an index of productivity, job satisfaction and commitment are not positively related to levels of employee productivity. A dissatisfied, burned-out, non-committed employee may very well be highly productive. In such an instance, there might be a fear of losing one's job, or maintaining a good work image to enhance one's chances of finding a better or more satisfying job elsewhere.

Overall, probably the vast majority of employees are motivated in some manner to produce at least enough to remain employed. Others produce much more; still others produce much less. The classic notion that about 20 percent of the employees produce about 80 percent of the work may not be too unrealistic. The individual's motivation, the climate of the organization, company philosophy, satisfaction and commitment facets, and other related factors are all interfaced in any given organization. The extent to which these components function in a complementary manner will either increase or decrease employee productivity as well as systems-wide productivity within the organization.

6

BARRIERS TO MOTIVATION AND PRODUCTIVITY

Some barriers have already been indicated in previous chapters. Barriers to motivation and productivity can be conceptualized as being both person- and system-based. In the person realm, socio-cultural, attitudinal, experiential, and perhaps metabolic phenomena contribute to one's motivation and productivity or the lack of it. Among systems, models which relate to traditions, budgetary issues, personality of the CEO, organizational climate, and management structure are foremost. A highly motivated employee can either be enhanced, thwarted, or destroyed by the system. On the other hand, a system can be progressive, slowed, or destroyed by employee power bases. Without the presence of functional symbiosis between employee and system, the structure will not be self-actualizing.

New employees always progress through various stages of adaptation to an organization. Such stages may include initial confusion (perhaps due to inadequate orientation), skepticism from other employees, assimilation into the culture, and later productivity and maturity. A conservative system may be well-oiled and perform in a passive manner due to the stabilizing forces of a core of tenured, power-base employees. When a system experiences sudden change (because of mandates from federal reviewers, for example), it may initially function as does the new employee. Sudden change in an organization is similar to our experience with coffee, oil and sugar shortages, or airline deregulation. The organizational "economy" is in a state of confusion while subsystems seek their own level of functioning. By addressing certain barriers, the reader should better relate to strategies by which to prevent such barriers.

COMMUNITY ROOTS, CULTURE, AND WORK ETHIC

Professionals (those with specialized technical degrees) and para-professionals (direct-care workers, support workers who characteristically do not have a four-year college degree as a requirement to practice their trade) generally inculcate different value systems in their work. HSOs cannot survive as a service or as a culture without the contributions of both.

Like it or not, HSOs function with a strong social class system, partly due to tradition. Paraprofessionals generally adhere to a strong sub-culture which may be off limits to the professionals, and vice versa. All things being equal, employees from academic categories such as high school and two-year college degree, baccalaureate, master's, doctoral, and key administrators (with a variety of degrees) generally do not cross class conceptual boundaries too often. Another way of categorizing employees would be that of exempt versus non-exempt personnel. Medical staff may establish barriers to other individuals even though certain professionals may be accepted into their domain. On the other hand, Naisbitt (1984) noted that such excellent companies as Intel had significantly informal organizational structures. In this trend, Naisbitt noted that the "new network" of informality, laterality, diagonality, and cross-disciplinary employee interactions would be the optimal management style of the future.

Part of the traditional class system of organizations is rooted in community systems and social classes. At the bottom of the social system is the "hound-dog group," as one of my undergraduate sociology professors noted. The extreme is the country club set. The hard-core unemployed (HCU) group may or may not include some of our people in low-level HSO jobs, especially at the PRFs. As I will note later regarding absenteeism and turnover, we may very well be pulling some of our employees from HCU ranks. As Triandis, Felden, Weldon, and Harvey (1975) noted, the HCU have historically been of minority status, low education, and poverty. Self-esteem is based upon factors other than holding a job. The HCU frequently have a distrust of systems, in that management is perceived to be in the business of taking advantage of the less fortunate. Searls, Bravelt, and Miskimins (1974) suggested that the HCU felt powerless and functioned under an external locus of control.

Paraprofessionals, perceived as second-class citizens by some, have traditionally been on the short end of the stick, so to speak. Constantly being "done to" rather than asked to input ideas, these individuals have been conditioned to distrust the system, offer passive resistance to productivity goals imposed upon them by administration, and have generally "seen programs come and go." Thaw and Wolfe (1986) suggested that the direct-care worker frequently perceived new behavioral programs and other treatment modalities as being just another requirement imposed upon them by a system which was already plagued with rules. In a job where significant stress and frustrations are ever-present, they noted that the direct-care worker's resistive behavior functioned as a self-protective device. Psychologists, social workers, case managers, team leaders, and QMRPs can be at the mercy of the direct-care worker who does not readily accept these professional philosophies and the behavioral expectations which they communicate.

Professionals, on the other hand, are busily competing for power, territory, and vested interests. In the end, the clients, patients, or inmates are not too much the worse for wear. As Thaw, Benjamin, and Cuvo (1986) noted, the professional has a specialized jargon and code of ethics which may serve to intimidate paraprofessionals. The use of implied and acquired power by the professional can further elicit stress and resistance from the direct-care worker. Other departments and position classes may be threatened, depending upon how well the professional handles this power. Historically, physicians gave orders, others made recommendations, and the direct-care workers and nurses followed orders. This picture is changing with the team approach to treatment, but ever so slowly.

Personality and behavioral structures of different employee groups can readily affect their co-workers and the clients or patients. (So, what else is new?) Seriously, there are issues of concern. For example, given a direct-care worker who has a myriad of family problems, lives in substandard housing, has a couple of junk cars in the yard, and who was picked up for Driving While Intoxicated or Driving Under the Influence (DWI or DUI) last month is not going to be exactly in an active-treatment mode at work. Or, take the person who periodically abuses his or her spouse or housemate. When this person (almost always unknown to the employer) inculcates violence into a lifestyle, then patient abuse and possible violence at work may occur. Here, one is dealing with a person who has low self-esteem and confidence and who may resort to aggressive behavior at home or at work when under high levels of stress. We may also have a person who is a compulsive worker as well as being an authoritarian manager; the result is obvious.

We have all encountered employees, regardless of their social position at work, who appear to be pre-programmed for a certain level of motivation and productivity. We see employees coming to work on time, going on break and to lunch at exact times, and generally "getting ready to quit" at about fifteen to thirty minutes before the end of their shift. On the other hand, almost all non-exempt employees follow these routines since twenty-four-hour care of clients or patients requires adequate and predictable employee coverage. Within this realm, we have the classic concept of work pacing. If one produces too little, one gets into trouble from the boss. If one produces too much, one's co-workers get excited since excessive productivity may show them up. As Parkinson (1957) classicly noted, "Work expands so as to fill the time available for its completion."

But, lest we become obsessed with attributing certain characteristics to employee lifestyles and behaviors, we may wish to adopt a positive philosophy, a self-fulfilling prophecy. As noted in Greek mythology, Pygmalion was a sculptor who carved a statue of a woman. In the process, he fell in love with it. Then, somewhat frustrated, he appealed to the Goddess of Love, Aphrodite, to instill life into the statue. Aphrodite granted his wish, and the woman was named Galatea (a sea nymph). Pygmalion made love to and finally married Galatea (Clark and Summers, 1975). Thus, one's expectancies can lead to an increase or decrease in another's level of performance.

SECURITY OF THE STATUS QUO

As stressed before, bureaucracies can become obsessed with the status quo. Change can be threatening to systems and to individuals within those systems. The CEO can promote or inhibit constructive change. As Daft and Becker (1978) suggested, executives could make change legitimate and valid. Thus, those CEOs who have a commitment to change the status quo will expend the needed effort to effect change. In the business and industry setting there is a notion that if a manager or executive does not accomplish significant things and move upward within about two to three years, then the person should probably seek opportunities elsewhere. New ideas are needed in an organization for progress and change to be realized. If the current employees can achieve this, well—fantastic! In many instances, however, recruiting outside personnel is one way to keep ideas flowing. In this respect, I dare say that if an organization does not have any key personnel with less than three years of tenure, then either they are exceptional employees or the organization is rapidly becoming stagnant.

Traditionally, top-heavy, centralized organizations have tended to be more rigid than those which have a wider power distribution. Hage (1980) noted that organizations which were decentralized, informal, and had employees with highly diverse skills had more capacity to innovate. Now, isn't this the climate of the HSOs? Yes, but internal power structures and occupational boundaries (often based upon educational status) may very well oppose innovation in practice. Hasenfeld (1983) noted, "As public bureaucracies, human service organizations are controlled by powerful interest groups who seek to maintain the status quo" (p. 218). Hasenfeld also suggested that since most HSOs lacked sufficient resources to generate profit, then any form of change would have involved more expenditures which were often unavailable. Change was also likely to upset the balance of power which further entrenched the need for status quo. Finally, it was suggested that those individuals who frequently resisted change and innovation generally only changed when under duress, as from external political pressures.

In PRFs, change can be extremely threatening. Just try to decentralize a system into autonomous units or divisions, which involves eliminating department heads! The resistance from managers can be as problematic as running through freshly poured concrete with oversized snowshoes. For example, in one organization, a system went from four units to three. One unit director was reassigned to an applied clinical role. The person resigned within one month. In another system, a new department head was hired to work with another well-entrenched department head as that person's supervisor. For months they were in conflict over turf issues.

From a psychological standpoint, the condition of status quo functions as security, safety, belongingness; micro-governments can occur within a system. People evolve to *own* their area and their supervisees. As long as one's role is not changed, then outsiders respect or support the person, regardless of their competence. Even if they *don't* respect or support the person or his/her ability, they probably have little influence or power to do anything about it. Additionally, the status quo implies that one does not have to improve oneself in order to maintain one's status. We all know of employees in power positions who are incompetent but whose power shields them from other people's forcing them to improve their education or knowledge. (More about this when matriarchs and patriarchs are discussed.)

Due in part to the phenomenon of cognitive dissonance, employees may attribute ulterior motives to management when change is advocated. As Sproull and Hofmeister (1986) noted, the alert manager will attempt to anticipate any potential problems regarding new organizational change. Once change is announced, the employees will have their own mental picture of its benefits and shortcomings—a picture that may or may not be the same as the manager's. Additionally, they suggested that when implementing new programs (change), the manager should anticipate possible problems (minimizing negative surprises) by admitting in advance that something might go wrong. On the other hand, the manager should structure change so that there were also some positive surprises, such as by not initially overselling the program components.

Finally, a status quo system (macro, mini, or micro) provides feedback to itself. It has a sort of looping, incestual relationship with itself. It is shielded from outside influence by the internal power structures. But when an external agent mandates change, confusion and chaos usually occur while the newly modified system is again seeking its own level of functioning.

SYSTEM ROADBLOCKS

As Hasenfeld (1983) suggested, HSOs were (and they still are) rather loosely integrated systems whereby departments and units do not always respond in a reciprocal manner. Chaotic environments, disruptive organizational climates, multiple vested interests and private agendas are frequently observed. The new wave of organizational technology is moving toward a decentralized, informal, communicative, and information-based structure (Naisbitt, 1984; Peters and Waterman, 1982; and Toffler, 1970). A carry-over from the baby-boom era which began to realize itself in the free sexuality of the 1960s and 1970s, it progressed through activist goals and a rethinking of societal issues and values. Individuals who grew up in that era have characteristically *networked* and as Naisbitt noted, this has been the dominant style of the new culture. And it is very dominant. The "old boy" networks were elitist if not sexist and were noted to be increasingly replaced in the new networking era. The impact was that by about 1990, some 80 percent of managers will be under the age of forty, and these managers will be advocating more participative management structures. The "Mr. Smith" or "J. B. Wilson" authority will be moving toward more "Mary," "Tom," and similar informalities.

The prior obsession with traditional organizational structures with their top-down authority lines is slowly eroding, but some significant roadblocks continue to be evidenced. These are noted next.

Bureaucratic Roadblocks

We have all heard, "You can't beat the system." Or, can you? A tenured Weberian bureaucrat loves the system. There is safety, predictability, and eventual status if for those who just "put in their 8" and wait for cost-of-living salary increases or promotions to roll around like the seasons of the year. These individuals do not like change, innovation, or anyone who rocks the boat. Any change in method, procedure, concept, or even a *form* can cause stress for these individuals. Festinger (1957), in discussing cognitive dissonance, suggested that any idea or information which was not in agreement with one's existing notions could produce dissonance, which could lead to stress and other anomalies of behavior. Thus, if the reward/punishment system was not sufficient to change the person's existing convictions, then there would be no motivation to change beliefs or behaviors.

A good bureaucrat goes by the rules and plays the game the expected way. Information may be power. Rigidity of thinking and the lack of ability to accept (and pursue) alternate courses of action may prevail. Recalling one situation in a PRF, there was a human resources administrator who apparently could not relate to an alternate way of obtaining needed positions for a department head (federal reviewers had requested that the facility increase positions in this area). There was a notion that position class numbers had already been allocated by the central office and a hierarchy of lengthy approvals and procedures as necessary to create a new and needed position. One rather resourceful external agency administrator suggested that a brief proposal be submitted to the chief of the human services division at the central office. The local administrator seemed to be shocked that anyone would suggest breaking the chain of command, even for a crisis!

Finally, people in bureaucratic systems have not been in the habit of doing things the efficient and expedient way. A hundred dollars will be spent to save ten. A number of years ago a ward at a psychiatric hospital needed a new door on a patient's room. Without the door, privacy was invaded and programming was disrupted. A work order was processed through channels. About a week later, the carpenter supervisor appeared and sized up the situation and took measurements.

A few days later, three workmen appeared: a carpenter, a helper, and a supervisor. By the end of the day the door had been hung. The ward supervisor asked why the door did not have a doorknob and latch. The supervisor remarked, "We only hang the door; the locksmith installs the latch." Then the door would have to be painted, etc., etc. A private carpenter contractor could have done the entire job in about four to six hours. In an ICF/MR facility, a door needed to be installed in a hallway to close off a newly designated aggressive behavior unit. The facility carpenters could not obtain a door at an area commercial lumber yard, because state bids had to be let. About six weeks later the door was up, using about four facility tradesmen. The list goes on forever.

The Organizational Underground

The underground can facilitate or destroy. Astute administrators have tapped into this employee network to gradually introduce new policy and procedural concepts. Inept administrators have failed to acknowledge this network and have allowed rumors and other dysfunctional employee behaviors to become rampant.

Dysfunctional underground processes can effectively block programming and disrupt the flow of treatment and system efficiency. The professional, supervisor, manager, or administrator who fails to tune in to this process can easily find him-or herself not being aware of the dynamics of the employees. The external person who communicates only downward or who has no allies in this network will never be fully aware of the organizational climate. Direct-service workers have a very powerful underground. It can be infiltrated and used as a mode of communication, but carefully and wisely. The building of trust relationships and two-way communication is essential. Sharing some "new" information with direct-service workers will facilitate this process. The person who is able to relate to a variety of individuals within the underground will be able to promote change and employee harmony, and will have an ongoing barometer of the *real* organizational climate. Generic attitude surveys may not elicit true feelings. If such surveys are conducted in a truly anonymous manner by someone who is trusted by the employees, then valid feelings and attitudes can be obtained.

Games Employees and Managers Play

Culture inculcates a model of gaming into people from an early age. We grow up with an expectancy of playing games as an avocation. The courtship game or ritual is common to all animal species. Employees and managers (as well as organizations) frequently play games. There is the status game or one-up-manship, evidenced by a bigger and better job or office, and the game of collecting employees to supervise. We also designate this as "achievement." Eric Berne (1964), in his best-selling book, *Games People Play*, described a variety of personal, social, and organizational games. Three of these seem appropriate for HSO climates:

The first is the game of Blemish. This, according to Berne, was the "I am no good" position and "They are no good" notion. In Freudian terms, this is the Parent-Child model. This can progress to authoritarian behavior (Adorno, Frenkel-Brunsurk, Lewinson, and Sandford, 1950). Berne also believed that the Blemish gamesperson was not satisfied until he or she could detect some fault in another in order to attribute some notion of inferiority. Once again, we have Pygmalion or attributional behavior.

The second was depicted by Berne as SWYMD. (Translated, "See What You Made Me Do.") In this paradigm, through a facade of democracy the manager will ask others for their input on something. If the suggestion fails to work, then the manager can attribute blame for failure to the person who made the suggestion. Management falsely becomes more omnipotent through the process of degrading others. Freud's position on this is relegated to the phallic stage of childhood development—when sexuality is emerging. Berne noted that SWYMD was analogous to premature ejaculation. He also suggested that this was related to Freud's notion of castration anxiety in the extreme. One does not engage a physician to perform circumcision who has a bad case of the D.T.'s.

NIGYSOB is also known as "Now I've Got You, You Son of a Bitch" (Berne, 1964). This is a very pragmatic and useful technique. It is the final coup of the Peter Principle (Peter and Hull, 1969) which classically and pessimistically notes that an employee is continually promoted for good performance until the employee can no longer perform effectively. Eric Berne noted that NIGYSOB was typical in the game of poker—when you deal yourself four aces. NIGYSOB is a two-handed game:

victim versus aggressor. It is "See, you have done wrong." You've done wrong; now you must be punished. This paradigm is similar to that found in the authoritarian pattern (Adorno et al., 1950) and McGregor's (1960) Theory X side of management. NIGYSOB is used by central offices and boards of directors when an HSO agency head screws up (or fails a state or federal certification review). It is scapegoating and witch-hunting. It can be an effective management tool to eventually remove incompetent or troublesome employees. Or, it can be one technique of the authoritarian manager.

NON-PRODUCTIVE EMPLOYEE BEHAVIORS

Matriarchs and Patriarchs

"Just tell it to Mother (or Daddy); I'll look out for your best interests. Be loyal to me and you will be cared for. [You may die in the process, but . . .]." Patriarchal/matriarchal individuals have "earned" their positions of power, regardless of competence. They are almost always long-tenured employees who are presently in mid-management positions. They rarely move to the CEO's office because external authorities would know what they are doing. I have known several such individuals, from facility superintendents down to first-line supervisors. As long as their turf is preserved, the remainder of the organization can do as it wishes. These individuals can also significantly block innovation and progress if it does not appear advantageous to them to change. They are like long-tenured college professors with full-professor status—I once overheard one full professor say, "I can do as I wish, I'm a Full Professor."

I remember one department head who played games such as removing the key to the copy machine so others could not use the copier. Another controlled the flow of paper by sitting on forms which needed a signature, perhaps as a power play. Appearing to "lose" paperwork is another ploy. The situation is controlled. Avoiding a reply to requests or not giving a response to a memo or phone call is another roadblock to productivity among matriarchs and patriarchs. Others may repeatedly make phone calls or send follow-up memos, but to no avail. One employee of mine, a long-tenured professional, effectively used this technique to control the situation, at least temporarily. Unless a higher-level supervisor communicates a requirement of efficiency, or uses other means to reduce or eliminate such roadblocks, then these methods will continue ad infinitum.

Learned Helplessness

As noted earlier, Seligman's (1975) work on learned helplessness is classic. Prior to that, Ewing (1967) made observations of cockroaches that give up and die when confronted with impossible odds against survival. Many of you have probably heard stories of dogs and other pets which have allegedly died of "grief" at the loss of their owner or other such phenomenon.

Helplessness among HSO personnel can develop as the result of repeated attempts to accomplish certain client or professional goals. These individuals may just stop trying to change the system or to achieve some goal. I propose that learned helplessness (due to failure to achieve work and personal goal actualization) can be a contributor to the status quo phenomenon. After months and years of trying to achieve a meaningful goal, the individual may resign him or herself to mediocrity and therefore add to the growing pool of statusquoism. For whatever reason, the individual remains on the job long enough to become entrenched into the culture of the local community; then, as the result of this heavy investment (financial and social), the individual gracefully slips into the employment rut. Other opportunities may be contemplated, even an occasional resume may be sent out in search for greener pastures. But, in the end, the individual decides to perseverate until the next employment anniversary date.

As this individual becomes deeper and deeper entrenched, vested interests become more established and slippage into a knowledge rut may very well occur. The organizational inbreeding continues.

Entrenchment into the popular culture of status quo can also lead to failure to try new things—informational atrophy. More and more mature potted plants and trinkets embellish the offices of those. On the other hand, should such individuals become so institutionalized that their careers have been up and down within the same organization, then anger, passive resistance, and even overt hostility and non-compliance with other employees may occur. Direct-service workers and professionals begin to merge in attitude and philosophy—a perspective of "the central office did it again," "the CEO is implementing another dumb idea," and so on, ad infinitum.

While there are no easy answers to learned helplessness, this attitude can be organizationally improved by the influx of new employees. The CEO must strive to recruit dynamic, innovative people with excellent people skills. It will take time, but attrition can win eventually. Conversely, with the private-sector HSOs which are not in the state merit system, helpless and status quo employees can be removed much more easily.

Psychological and Behavioral Withdrawal and Round Tuits

In this paradigm, employees who have experienced a variety of defeats and castigations will either leave the organization, become further entrenched into the status quo, or perhaps actively fight back in a passive-aggressive manner. As previously indicated, passive-aggressive behaviors can include obstructionism, delays in the flow of routine business functions, and related behaviors. Some employees may suddenly "wake up" just before payday. I have known several who have fifteen or twenty years of tenure with an organization and, following a series of ups and downs over the years, have essentially resigned themselves to fate.

Some simply stop trying to change the system; others fail to respond to requests by others. Typical reactions are "Oh, did you send it to me—it must have gotten lost," or "The project is nearly finished—I'll send it right over." Both involve excuse-making for something that was never begun in the first place.

The *Round Tuit* is the tool of the procrastinator. It can be either by design or due to poor time management on the part of the employee. These people never seem to get their act together. They're always going to get *around to it*. They may be simply absentminded or, in the more severe cases, inefficient and not cost-effective to the organization. It can also be a technique used by a committee. In such paradigms, the committee chair may say, "Your request has been taken under advisement," or "The committee will get back to you soon." Both may use either a model of filibustering or one of passive-aggressive behavior to extinguish someone else's behavior for whatever reason.

Absenteeism and Turnover

Steers and Rhodes (1978) noted that industrial losses due to absenteeism amounted to about $26 billion per year. The Bureau of National

Affairs (Bureau, 1974) surveyed 200 companies and found that about 75 percent of the managers reported that absenteeism was their most serious disciplinary problem.

Here, we have the most severe systems issue facing HSOs apart from budgetary constraints. As a service-based business, HSOs probably have upwards to 80 percent of their budgets encumbered for personnel and related object codes. In a pilot survey of a hundred randomly selected HSO facilities in the United States (thirty responded, for a non-statistically significant sample), Martin (1987) reported turnover rates of between about 20 and 60 percent. In fact, one PRF had experienced an extremely high turnover rate of about 90 percent among direct-service workers and technicians, with over 50 percent turnover for some key support positions such as dieticians, speech and hearing pathologists, and physical therapists. Additionally, despite premium pay and shift differential for registered nurses (RNs) and licensed practical nurses (LPNs), a 25 to 50 percent vacancy rate remained for months.

Abelson (1987) surveyed nursing personnel from five nursing homes in rural settings. Facility sizes ranged between 120 and 242 beds. Respondents (191) included registered nurses, licensed practical nurses, and nursing aides. At the end of one year, 136 remained employed, 9 had left involuntarily, 30 had left for avoidable and 16 for unavoidable reasons; this represented about a 29 percent turnover rate among the leavers. Results suggested that avoidable leavers were less satisfied and less committed to the organization than stayers. Job tension and withdrawal cognition (e.g., thinking of quitting or intent to search) was also noted as being higher for avoidable leavers than for stayers.

In studying technician turnover and absenteeism at public residential facilities, Zaharia and Baumeister (1978) noted that as of about 1978, formal studies investigating the dollar costs of turnover in PRFs were essentially nonexistent. They suggested that the replacement costs for one direct-care worker was about $1,563. *Leavers* were generally younger, better educated, under twenty-four years old at job entry, had been on the job less than four months, and in the state less than six years. On the other hand, *stayers* tended to be less educated, wanted any type of work, had lived in the state most of their lives, and may be minority persons. Some causes of turnover were indicated to be issues such as wage scales, not reporting for work at the onset, the feeling that the PRF job was of low social status, finding a better job elsewhere, dissatisfaction with management, and personal factors.

In regard to the association between absenteeism and turnover, Porter and Steers (1973) noted that absenteeism was generally negatively correlated with turnover. Jewman (1974) failed to find a positive relationship between co-worker satisfaction and absenteeism. Steers and Rhodes (1978) suggested that there were two forms of absenteeism: involuntary and voluntary. Involuntary included illness, injury, and other factors. Voluntary included any type of unauthorized absence from work. Abelson (1987) discussed *avoidable* and *unavoidable* turnover. Avoidable turnover was identified as that which was under the control of the employee; unavoidable was turnover due to such situations as death or illness. The relationship between employee turnover and performance was studied by Cope, Grossnickle, Covington, and Durham (1987) among 144 leavers and 144 stayers across thirty-two positions in a facility for the mentally retarded. Results indicated that performance ratings were lower for leavers than for stayers, especially among the direct-care workers at the facility. Markham, Dansereau, and Alutto (1982) investigated work-group size and absenteeism rates through longitudinal retrospective correlational analysis. They found that among 1,300 workers at a manufacturing plant, absenteeism was higher among those employees in large work groups than for those working in small groups.

Addressing the Absenteeism Issue

When cash bonuses of forty hours' pay were given for six months of perfect attendance, absenteeism decreased by about 34 percent (Grove, 1968). Lawler and Hackman (1969) found a significant reduction in absenteeism for several work groups of sixty-six maintenance workers which were allowed to help design a program for absence reduction as opposed to management's imposing a system upon employees. In another study of about seventy-five employees at an ICF/MR, use of a peer-group contingent to reinforce acceptable levels of attendance and schedule approved time-off resulted in significant reductions in absenteeism (Reid, Schuh-Wear, and Brannon, 1978). Among about thirty-two workers at an ICF/MR facility, no significant change in sick days was found following the introduction of a four-day workweek (Pierce, Hoffman, and Pelletier, 1974). Use of flexitime among eighty-four professional and hourly employees produced some improvement in worker attendance (Golembiewski, Hilles, and Kagno, 1974). In a review of about seven studies on flexitime and four-day workweeks, the author concluded that flexitime had a better effect on absenteeism (Durand, 1986).

Use of a cash lottery drawing for a monthly amount of $10 (1976 value) was implemented for eighty production and office workers for one month's perfect attendance. This method, according to Wallin and Johnson (1976) produced about a 30 percent reduction in absenteeism. A small study of fifteen institutional workers with a history of chronic absenteeism involved techniques of supervisory counseling, commendation letters, and a behavioral lottery. Absenteeism was reduced in eleven of the fifteen workers (Shoemaker and Reid, 1980). In these respects, this author is aware of another facility which used the lottery system and it backfired.

In a rather large study of about 7,500 production workers at two large manufacturing plants, Kempen and Hall (1977) reported about a 30 percent reduction in absenteeism using organizational behavior management (OBM) techniques. Here, a series of graduated warnings leading to termination was the punisher. Reinforcement for acceptable attendance included removing the time clock, time off with pay, and immunity from punishers for a stated period of time. For better attendance at meetings in an HSO, public posting was used to display graphs of attendance records. Absenteeism was reduced (Hutchison, Jarman, and Bailey, 1980). Jackson (1983) studied about 126 hospital personnel using a multiple group control design. Staff attendance at meetings was doubled. No significant change in absenteeism rates was observed when workers attended more meetings.

Using a rather involved paradigm, Ford (1981) used simple punishment (OBM) to reduce absenteeism some. Here, the supervisor called the employees absent from work, asked them to report in detail the nature of their absence, the expected duration of the absence, and in case of medical reasons, the details of the treatment. They were also asked to indicate any items that needed to be done during their absence. Finally, the supervisor emphasized the burden that the absence placed upon their co-workers. This technique was tried by an administrative person at one facility where the author worked. Results produced negative reactions among the employees and certain amounts of passive-aggressive behavior. The system, according to the author's information, was terminated soon after.

On the positive side, feedback plus feedback and social reinforcement (OBM) was used for attendance improvement among about twenty female office workers. Public posting of attendance significantly reduced absenteeism. Durand (1983) used a method of the same type as did Lawler and Hackman (1969) to reduce absenteeism. At an institution for the mentally retarded, Durand (1983) allowed about seventeen workers to design their own invervention for absenteeism. Absence-free for one month, the employee could earn eight hours of time off. The absenteeism rate decreased from about 8.6 to about 5.3 percent with maintenance continuing for at least twelve months.

Various methods have been used to address the absenteeism issue at HSOs and in the business and industry setting. Not all of the studies used appropriate statistical designs or sufficient sample sizes, but there appears to be some evidence for the use of peer-designed absenteeism policies and the use of cash awards and time off for rewarding good work attendance. Of course, any such award systems should be based on reinforcers which the employees perceive to have an equitable value for effort.

7

HUMAN FACTORS AND PERFORMANCE

Human factors, or what some have called ergonomics or human engineering, is a key concept with any organization. Essentially, it is the *fit between people, jobs, tools, equipment, and the work environment.* For centuries, people attempted to improve the methods by which they did work, and improved the equipment, machines, and environment in which the work was done. Not until recent decades has the area of human factors been studied from a scientific standpoint. In the early part of the twentieth century, Taylor (1903) introduced the concept of *time study* while Gilbreth and Gilbreth (1921) discussed the concept of *motion study.*

According to Chapanis (1983), engineering psychology is synonymous with human factors. In effect, engineering psychology involves the discovery and application of information about human behavior in relation to the equipment, tools, type of job, and work environment in which a given job is performed. It is the logical outgrowth of the earlier concepts of man and machine systems postulated by Munsterberg (1913). As previously mentioned, during the era of the Hawthorne studies (Roethlisberger and Dickson, 1939), the issue of worker versus system interaction gained momentum. McCormick and Ilgen (1985) noted that the area of human factors received significant impetus during World War II as the result of problems encountered in the operation and maintenance of new military equipment.

Three systems were conceptualized by McGrath (1983) in the area of human factors. *System A*—the physical and technological environment where worker behavior occurs; *System B*—social interactions of the workers; and *System C*—the "person" or "self" system of the individual worker. These systems further encompass behavior settings, organizational tasks, organizational roles, and the actual behavior of the employee in the organization.

Bandura (1978) postulated the notion of *reciprocal determinism*. It suggested that while the environment might influence the worker's behavior, the worker's behavior could also create or influence the environment. Going further, Weick (1979) noted there was also an *enactment process* where the individual actively influenced the environment. Additionally, the individual responded to the *created* environment rather than to the actual environment. McGrath, Bandura, and Weick each addressed very similar concepts as they related to the people/environment/job interaction.

THE PEOPLE AND THE JOB FIT

Perhaps the easiest way to conceive of the people/job fit is that the employee should interface with his or her job and the job environment if optimal functioning and productivity are to occur. Hopefully, this is the role of the facility's human resources department. But, as we well know, there are instances where a "warm body" must be assigned to a treatment ward or other work area.

On the other hand, the selection of people to fill a job in the professional area is probably done the most scientifically since a high degree of responsibility and cost-benefit is at stake. With the PRFs, this is not always the case. It is not unusual for a PRF to go on a massive recruitment effort as the result of the threat of decertification following an HCFA review. Aides are placed in aide jobs, nurses in nurse jobs, and case managers or QMRPs are placed in those jobs. When push comes to shove, a warm body is better than losing millions of dollars in federal Medicare/Medicaid funds—or is it?

Ideally, in an acute or chronic psychiatric hospital, in an aggressive behavior unit in a mental retardation facility, or in a correctional facility, there is a notion that an ablebodied person who has skills in behavior intervention is the ideal candidate. But, this does not always happen. I have seen less than physically able aides assigned to wards where patient behaviors accelerated on a regular basis—and injuries to less able staff occurred.

In the PRFs, the hiring is controlled by the civil service register, and jobs are frequently assigned on the basis of the highest score. Internal transfers may be based on seniority rather than qualifications, but people/job fit issues are also considered. Cynical? Yes. I have seen too many people hired due to an urgent need to fill a position without too much concern for the person's ability to relate psychologically or socially to the work environment. Some examples follow.

First, I have seen psychologists and other professionals hired who had significant dysfunctional personalities which were exacerbated by the demanding environment of the institutional setting. In a few cases, significantly passive-aggressive people have been employed. Second, there have been physicians hired who had only minimal knowledge of the institutional use of psychotropic medications. Third, a dentist believed that patients in an institution did not feel as much pain as did a "normal" person; anesthetic was generally not given. He was later fired following a federal survey. Fourth, the people/job fit is also moderated by the concept of seniority. Tenure can become the qualification for a promotion rather than competence.

There is a significant need to better match individuals with the job in our PRFs. In the nursing homes, which are also under scrutiny, competent employees are difficult to find. Our general hospitals and community mental health centers have a better fit of people to jobs, primarily because there has been considerable competition for those jobs and better screening. Correctional facilities could also do better. Our halfway houses and community-based mental retardation and psychiatric living centers do not always have competent staff to work with these transitional clients. One reason is that the pay is rather poor, along with these jobs having less prestige than some others.

We need to recruit, hire, and place employees who are better able to cope with the demands and stressors of HSO jobs. One way is to do better screening of job applicants for social and personality dynamics. Another is to increase salaries and improve the organizational climate so that employees with more competence and, it is hoped, better social skills can be hired. Additionally, the PRFs must strive to obtain better funding for their programs and improve the work environment (physically and socially). The state civil service systems need a work-over. The examination basis for hiring precludes screening out individuals who do not psychologically fit the climate of human services. Salaries and benefits must be made competitive with private-sector facilities as well as with industry. Job security is not enough to retain competent employees. They also need some good perks.

STRESS AND THE ENVIRONMENT

The effects of acute or chronic stress have been related to temporary or chronic psychosomatic reactions of the individual. In his pioneering work on homeostasis, Walter B. Cannon used the term *stress* to describe various emotional states which could have an effect on the physiological functioning of an organism (Cannon, 1914). Later, Cannon (1935) suggested that stress included phsyical stimuli and that *strain* was the organism's response. The most popular notion of stress was postulated by Hans Selye through his concept of the General Adaptation Syndrome (GAS) in that the GAS was the body's response to prolonged adverse circumstances (Selye, 1956).

Selye described three major stages of a stress response: alarm, resistance, and exhaustion. In the *alarm* mode, a chain reaction of physiological processes occurs. First, demands upon the individual signal the body to prepare for action. The individual may decide to either attack or retreat from the perceived stressor. Second, the hypothalamus in the brain activates the sympathetic division of the autonomic nervous system to act. Third, the body is readied to combat the stress. Fourth, the epinephrine and norepinephrine are released. Fourth, the hypothalamus activates the anterior pituitary and other hormones are released. Sixth, adrenocorticotropic hormone (ACTH) is released. Seventh, the adrenal cortex releases corticoids. Eighth, the organism's glucose level increases and mineralcorticoids help regulate sodium and potassium levels. The second major stage of stress is *resistance*. Assuming that the individual has not warded off the stress response at this point, the psychosomatic response occurs which can include changes in bodily tissue. Finally, in the *exhaustion* stage, coma and/or death can occur.

STRESS AND THE EMPLOYEE

McGrath (1983) noted that "stress involves an interaction of person and environment" (p. 1352). McGrath also suggested that stress could result from tasks, roles, behavior settings, physical environments, and within the person. Environmental stressors included extreme heat or cold, specific physical hazards, noise, and demands of the work in the context of the environment. In a literature review of issues in job stress, employee health, and organizational effectiveness, Beehr and Newman (1978) noted that both personal and environmental facets were involved in stressful situations. Four approaches to the study of occupational stress were postulated by Beehr and Franz (1987): medical psychology, clinical and counseling psychology, engineering psychology, and organizational psychology.

Kahn, Wolfe, Quinn, Snock, and Rosenthal (1964) surveyed employees in a nationwide study and found that about one-third of the respondents reported some form of occupational stress. An early analysis of acute stressors—personal, job-related, and environmental—was done by Holmes and Rahe (1967) using their Social Readjustment Rating Scale. A variety of stressors were ranked on a scale between 11 and 100. On their scale, being fired at work had a rating of 47, changing jobs was rated 36, and having trouble with one's boss had a rating of 23. Death of a spouse received a rating of 100. We know that all stress is not necessarily bad. In some instances, a moderate amount of stress can motivate certain individuals toward more productive behavior. However, like pain, stress appears to be relative to the individual. In relating *Type A* behavior (driving, coronary-prone individuals) to stress, Friedman and Rosenman (1974) noted that some Type A individuals appeared to thrive on stress and did not seek to protect themselves from stressors.

The concepts of *negative affectivity* (NA) and *positive affectivity* (PA) were proposed by Watson, Pennebaker, and Folger (1987). Individuals who experienced NA patterns reported a higher level of stress, distress, and physical complaints even if there was an absence of objective stressors. On the other hand, the PA individuals reported positive feelings about themselves and their lives in general.

In a review of studies dealing with acute and chronic stressors in the work environment, Greenhaus and Parasuraman (1987) noted that both work and non-work stressors had an additive effect. Acute stressors included job changes, transfers, and layoffs. Chronic stressors related to one's role in the organization as well as work overload. Non-work stressors included personal and family illness, death in the family, divorce, change of residence, household problems, financial problems, a low self-concept, and dissatisfaction with one's leisure. Kahn et al. (1964) also noted the existence of both role ambiguity and role conflict.

Work-related stressors were also summarized by Ivancevich and Matteson (1980) and Cooper and Marshall (1976). These included role conflict and ambiguity, work overload, problems with interpersonal relationships, dysfunctional organizational structures, lack of career path opportunities, as well as noise, temperature, and safety hazards. Employees may experience symptoms such as job dissatisfaction, tension, anxiety, depression, boredom, fatigue, and alienation. Some behavioral consequences could include increased smoking and drug/alcohol use, lowered job performance, absenteeism, and turnover. Cardiovascular and gastrointestinal problems have also been noted.

WORK SCHEDULES AND ROTATIONS

The first study to investigate the effects of paced versus non-paced work was conducted by Conrod (1955), who studied workers engaged in a packing task. Paced work, such as in assembly-line or other routine and non-creative work was noted by Hurrell and Colligan (1987) to increase levels of anxiety and depression among affected workers. Non-paced (self-directed) work seemed to produce fewer negative psychological affects upon its employees.

Shiftwork has generally been observed to variously affect one's day-night cycle, the circadian (based on the Latin meaning "about day") rhythm. Humans are not characteristically nocturnal in their cycles. The biological clock seems to be internally rather than externally generated. Humans' circadian rhythms appear to be regulated by the pineal gland in the brain which releases large amounts of melatonin at night and small amounts in the daytime. High levels of melatonin apparently promote sleep. The presence of light appears to inhibit the production of melatonin in the daytime and "resets" the biological clock. The presence of sightedness or lack of it does not appear to affect the clock.

At night one's body temperature gradually lowers until just before normal daytime awakening (Kalat, 1984). The effects of one's circadian rhythms upon shiftwork was noted by Hurrell and Colligan (1987). They noted that one's body temperature was lowest at about 4:00 A.M., rapidly increasing until about six to eight o'clock in the morning. One's temperature was reported to be at a peak at about 6:00 P.M.. Furthermore, due to these normal rhythms, night workers reported receiving less sleep than day workers despite their attempts to obtain adequate sleep. Some night workers reported increased gastrointestinal problems; however, there does not appear to be a symptom profile as yet.

EMPLOYEE STRESS, THE ENVIRONMENT, AND BURNOUT

Individuals who work with psychiatric, mentally retarded, nursing home, and offender populations experience considerable stress from the service delivery, environmental, and clientele standpoints. In the general hospitals, private-sector psychiatric hospitals, and community mental health centers, the decorum of the environment tends to be better than average. The outpatient facilities associated with the medical schools and the more prestigious private facilities are in the minority from the standpoint of having a significant positive environment. Since these facilities tend to generate revenue from their patients as well as from federal and third-party insurance reimbursements, there are more discretionary dollars to use. In the community-based mental retardation, drug and alcohol detoxification, sheltered workshop, and nursing home environments, the funds to provide positive environmental climates are not always available. A large number of these latter facilites are using makeshift buildings which have been converted from former business buildings and private residences.

The majority of the PRFs which are housed in nineteenth-century institutional structures are undoubtedly the worst in terms of appropriate and normalized structures. These old buildings were originally designed to warehouse hundreds of patients in an economy-of-scale, custodial model. Not only are these structures obsolete, many are in need of continual repairs in order to comply with fire and safety codes. Even newer buildings constructed as late as the 1950s do not facilitate proactive treatment and rehabilitation.

Turkington (1985) suggested that women were burning out at alarming rates across the country. Part of this appeared to be due to their having dual roles (homemaker and employee). This has led to increased demands upon their time and an increase in stress levels. In what has historically been known as a man's world in business, women have experienced additional stress as the result of having to compete in this environment.

In addressing role loss, Schlenkar and Gutek (1987) conducted a naturalistic study of 180 social workers at a large public services agency who had been involuntarily reassigned within the agency due to a budget crunch (data from 132 individuals were analyzed). The reassignments resulted in demotions of the employees from the professional position of social worker to non-professional casework positions. The acute stress reaction of these individuals was similar to that experienced by persons who become unemployed. Nine months later, there was evidence that the reassigned social workers had "adapted" to their new roles even though those roles had little value for them. They continued to identify with the social worker role, with increased intention of looking for another job.

Burnout has been defined as emotional exhaustion which resulted from the stressors of interpersonal interactions (Maslach, 1976, 1978). Furthermore, Pines and Aronson (1981) believed that burnout included a variety of exhaustion reactions which resulted from repeated interpersonal pressures over an extended period of time. For example, two instruments (among others) have been used to measure the construct of burnout. These have included the Maslach Burnout Inventory (Maslach and Jackson, 1981), and the Staff Burnout Scale for Health Professionals (Jones, 1980). Both appear to have some promises for measuring the construct of burnout in a valid and reliable manner.

Some observations made by Jones (1982) are noted. First, some burned-out workers seemed to come to work under the influence of alcohol (or hung over) more than did those who were not defined as burned-out. Among those employees classified as burned-out, more instances of argumentative behavior, on-the-job mistakes, and counter-productivity were noted. Working undesirable shifts also seemed to contribute to burnout. More job turnover, absenteeism, and tardiness were also related to higher levels of measured burnout. Jones also found that burned-out nurses reported a higher degree of drug theft than did non-burned-out nurses.

It is difficult to separate stress from burnout. Both seem to co-vary to a certain degree. Burned-out employees appear to display a sense of hopelessness and frustration with the job. Employees experiencing an acute or chronic mode of stress may or may not be experiencing burnout.

According to Matteson and Ivancevich (1982), tens of millions of American workers are experiencing job-related stress. Even if the normal workweek is forty hours, the peripheral time which includes going to and from work and the taking home of unfinished work can easily turn the usual workday into eleven or twelve hours. It was also noted that individuals experiencing stress tended to make more errors, were absent more, were less creative, and were less effective decision-makers than those not experiencing stress reactions. The authors indicated that while the actual dollar cost of employee stress is unknown, it has been estimated at around $75 to 90 billion annually, over three times that attributed to alcoholism.

To exemplify the plight of the direct-care workers, the following was written by a direct-service worker at a state institution.

> The employee morale at ――― is very low. Each day they are faced with high stress, high noise levels, more often than not, short staffing ... They are expected to be loving, kind, mild tempered, liberal with praise for the clients. Many function in areas where physical injury is possible. [They] deal with life threatening situations in the form of seizures, choking, ill, aggression, attack

staff and one another.... They receive comparatively low wages for the stress and risk involved. Absenteeism is high, nerves frayed, tempers are short, and personality conflicts common.

Another area of friction was the lack of communication.... There also seems to be a favoring of shifts. Third shift is almost unanimous in saying they were the last informed. That they were the ones expected to clean up after the others. They receive precious little information about changes in programs, and the ones they do receive are not always followed by the other shifts.

This writer could not have expressed the above comments better. If the above conditions fail to produce stress and morale problems among the direct service worker, well, probably nothing will short of an earthquake.

PERSONAL PROBLEMS AND ILLNESS

In addition to the usual stresses of working with emotionally disturbed and/or mentally retarded individuals in the institutional setting, direct-service workers have a variety of additional problems. These individuals are in the front line of treatment and frequently are the victims of aggressive advances from patients. Professionals are too frequently unavailable (or unwilling) to assist with these altercations, especially when they occur on the late-night, 11 to 7 shift.

The direct-service worker is also in the forefront of custodial care functions, such as cleaning up after a patient becomes incontinent or regurgitates. In the institutional setting serving nursing care or severely and profoundly mentally retarded patients, the direct-service worker must also attend to personal care (e.g., bathing, showering, or toileting) of a patient who may or may not be aggressive. There is the notion that one can sometimes identify a direct-care worker by the presence of bruises, cuts, scratches, and torn clothes. Should a direct-service worker (or other employee) have experienced personal problems outside of the work environment, then the job setting tends to exacerbate these problems. If the direct-service worker reaches the "breaking point" following a series of stressors and inadvertently abuses a patient, then the system puts full blame on the "weakness" of the direct-service worker without addressing the cumulative effect of personal and job-related stressors.

Direct-service workers and others who work in low-paying institutional jobs do not always practice proper medical care and nutrition on and off the job. Even with a good company-paid health care plan the worker may not always have the necessary funds to pay the deductible or to purchase medication and supplies. (But, some good medical plans have minimum co-payment charges.) Eating habits are not the best at home or at work. When the PRF does not provide protected lunch breaks, then the direct-service worker must grab a bite to eat on the run, usually junk food. These stressors can add to the ongoing demands of the job.

Problems with baby-sitters, being a single parent, lack of funds to enroll their children in a good daycare center, unreliable transportation to and from work, finances, and substance abuse can further increase the stress level of the direct-service worker. The employer does not always acknowledge or address these issues.

Whether the employee in an HSO (especially the PRF) is a direct-service worker or professional, the stressors of the job can accumulate to the point that the person may very well become psychosomatically ill. While the medical cause may be less direct, there is the notion that when a person is under a significant amount of stress as the result of both personal and job-related problems the individual may in fact become medically ill.

Professionals, too, are not exempt from workplace stressors in the HSOs. Generally, these take the form of conflicting messages from administration and the central office or other governing board or agency. Goals are not always clearly defined, and professionals frequently have to second guess the regulations. Among co-workers, the professionals are frequently involved with territorial issues and private agendas. If an outsider enters their turf—well, beware! Professionals in HSOs *should* be the most qualified to incorporate the niceties of positive reinforcement and other human relations perks. This is not always the case. Feedback, praise, and recognition are often replaced with distance and extinction. If a professional happens to be working at a facility (or job area) that was not the individual's first choice as an employer, then lowered self-esteem, defensiveness, and perhaps resentment may occur. Passive-aggressive behavior may occur. Obstructionism and paperwork sabotage may occur as frustrations increase. The professional may or may not exhibit increased absenteeism or tardiness as the result of stress, since there may be more professional identity and commitment than with the direct-service workers (but not always). Griping, back-stabbing, and other negative behaviors may be substituted for absenteeism. A lack of creativity and spontaneity may be present as the burned-out professional merely "puts in 8" to earn the predictable paycheck.

SUBSTANCE ABUSE

In recent years there has been a significant increase in the amount of substance abuse practiced among American citizens. Cocaine has become the affluent worker's drug of leisure. Alcohol use has continued at predictable rates. Marijuana and hashish have diminished some in use since their popularity of the 1960s and 1970s. The use of prescription drugs such as the amphetamines (mood elevators) and barbiturates (mood depressants) as well as the minor tranquilizers has been continuing. Employees in medical service areas such as physicians, nurses, medication aides, and others are suspected of using these drugs more than the general public, due to the ready availability of the drugs. Direct-service workers have been known to report to work under the influence of alcohol, marijuana, and cocaine. Some employees partake of these substances while at work, during their breaks.

During the past five to ten years, it has become increasingly unpopular for individuals to smoke over-the-counter tobacco products, mostly due to the issue of second-hand smoke and related health problems. A number of state and federal employers have implemented stringent non-smoking environments in the workplace, as have many in the private sector. It is increasingly becoming a sin to smoke, chew, or dip tobacco. Up until about the mid-to-late 1970s, smokers were tolerated but rarely punished for their habit. The non-smoker cannot conceive of why anyone would want to use tobacco. The smoker has a valid addiction to nicotine as well as a psychological habituation. When the tobacco user is prohibited from smoking in many workplace settings, this can cause significant stress reactions. This can also lead to the individual sneaking away to partake of tobacco. When the tobacco user is denied free use of tobacco, then the resulting anxiety can reduce mental alertness, work efficiency, and emotional stability. There are no easy answers.

8

INCREASING MOTIVATION AND PRODUCTIVITY

For a number of decades American and foreign managers have sought to improve the motivation and productivity of their employees. Hopkins and Sears (1982) reviewed twenty-eight studies which related to productivity improvement; nine related to productivity in human services. Those in human services reported an increase in productivity which ranged between 23 and 425 percent. Among the nineteen in the business and industry setting, increases ranged between 3 and 178 percent with one study reporting a 90 percent *decrease* in productivity. Reinforcement methods for the twenty-eight studies included individual and group feedback, graphic charts, cash bonuses, token reinforcement program, social reinforcement, paid time off, verbal praise, lottery, and others. This was only a sampling of the many studies conducted on the subject of productivity. Even today, there does not appear to be a panacea method to increase productivity.

The field of industrial and organizational psychology and its utility for dealing with employee behaviors has roots in management theory. The early work of Frederick W. Taylor (Taylor, 1911), which dealt with improving the efficiency of certain tasks in assembly-line production, provided significant impetus to managing employee behavior on a scientific basis. Taylor's work significantly influenced the work of Hugo Munsterberg (Munsterberg, 1913), who applied the principles of psychology to management in the industrial setting. As previously noted, the classic Hawthorne studies at Western Electric (Roethlisberger and Dickson, 1939) were seminal in stimulating the industrial relations movement in business and industry.

Both the private-sector business and industry setting and the public-sector human services environment have similar problems as well as needs in the area of effective human resources management. Both are ultimately concerned with the greatest return on the investment of human resources, materials, supplies, and equipment. While the public- or private-sector HSO macrosystem does not always acknowledge to its employees or to the public that they are involved with a units-of-production (service) phenomenon, it is a reality. No business enterprise, product or service, can survive very long without its balance sheet being in balance. Deficit spending is not the best management practice whether you are producing widgets or rehabilitating patients. A rather realistic view of the nature of human services (mental health, mental retardation, and corrections) was noted by Christian and Hannah (1983):

> There may be no industry in greater need of effective management than the human service system. Escalating costs, increasing governmental regulation, and persistent consumer demand have created an industry that appears actively to resist direction and control. Our technology for developing service delivery systems has surpassed our technology for effectively managing them (p. 1).

Christian and Hannah (1983) also noted that the managers' transition from theory to practice was often difficult due to a plethora of theories on motivation. They also suggested that managers' formal education and HSO experiences did not always prepare them to serve the many demands of their HSO managerial role. Managers were frequently oriented to a top-down managerial style and one which was often reactive rather than proactive. Such styles were also suggested to result in poor staff morale and lowered productivity.

American business has experienced less than optimal productivity in recent years. The causes include both macro- and micro-economic phenomena. The international business enterprise climate significantly influences these productivity levels. While the HSO setting is not so acutely influenced by business and industry practices per se, HSOs are affected by the cost of supplies, equipment, building construction, and personnel. As I have indicated before, HSOs are not cost-effective environments, especially those operated under governmental control, such as the PRFs. Additionally, the federal influence of the HCFA further serves to reduce their cost-effectiveness with continually increasing quality assurance requirements rooted in patients' rights. No one will argue with the need for proactive treatment of patients in a safe, human rights–oriented environment. But these increased demands have caused considerable confusion over service delivery models and how to finance them. It is extremely difficult to measure productivity among HSO workers when performance goals are ill-defined and criteria for patient treatment success are nebulous. We can measure the dollar cost of absenteeism and spoiled supplies, but I am not sure we can easily measure treatment cost-benefit among patients in long-term care institutional settings. Hopkins and Sears (1982) indicated that most of the public-sector research on productivity has investigated the direct observation of employee behavior, while the business research has concentrated on units-of-production measures.

There are some well-managed private-sector businesses and some poorly run ones. The same holds true for both private- and public-sector HSOs. The majority of the public-sector institutions (PRFs) are victims of federal regulations and state priorities. Policies, programs, and management staffs are frequently reactionary in their attempt to cope with increasing numbers of regulations and mandates. Competent employees are difficult to recruit for the PRFs. If an employee remains six months to a year and obtains tenure, then the issue of motivation and productivity seems to take a back seat to the reactionary nature of the business at hand. The field of human services should be the best-equipped to successfully motivate its employees to higher levels of productivity, since the nature of the business is rooted in the principles of psychology, especially learning theory. However, something seems to break down in the rush to be all things to all people.

ORGANIZATIONAL BEHAVIOR MANAGEMENT

The concept of organizational behavior management (OBM) has its origins in management principles and learning theory (Frederiksen, 1980, 1981, 1982). During the active influences of Sigmund Freud and Charles Darwin about the turn of the twentieth century, behaviorism held a significant role. These individuals subscribed to a notion that behavior was somewhat deterministic; Freud believed that humans had primarily two motivations, work and love. Kazdin (1978) noted that OBM evolved from early concepts of behavioral determinism. Ivan Pavlov (1849–1936), a Russian physiologist, is famous for his model of reflexive behavior which demonstrated that animal behavior could be conditioned to respond to a variety of primary and secondary stimuli. Pavlov believed that behavior was due to external conditions as opposed to Freud's notion that behavior was largely due to unconscious motivations. Behaviorism as a school of psychology is generally considered to have originated with John B. Watson (1878–1958) around 1913 (Hilgard and Bower, 1966).

Another important contributor to the issue of behaviorism and its implications for motivation was Edward C. Tolman (1886–1959). Tolman's classic work, *Purposive Behavior in Animals and Men* (Tolman, 1932), postulated a pure form of behaviorism wherein he rigidly rejected any form of cognitive introspection as a determinate of behavior. Tolman believed that behavior involved *molar* concepts and that behavior was *goal-directed*. Additionally, behavior was viewed as incorporating the environmental constructs in the means-to-end directions of the individual. Behavior was believed to pursue the "principle of least effort" and to be teachable. Rewards and punishers were perceived to regulate performance.

The classic notion that an individual would repeat those behaviors which were perceived by the individual to be rewarding or pleasurable, the law of effect was proposed by Edward L. Thorndike (1874–1949). Rewards or successes would therefore serve to further the learning of the rewarded behavior while, on the other hand, punishers or failures would reduce the individual's tendency to repeat the behavior (Hilgard and Bower, 1966).

B. F. Skinner described his theories of *operant conditioning* in his *Behavior of Organisms* (Skinner, 1938). Based upon the works of Pavlov, Watson, Thorndike, and others, Skinner's concepts emphasized *observable and measurable* behavior. During about the 1950s and 1960s, Skinner's concepts of operant conditioning were redirected from the animal research laboratories to human applications under the designation of *behavior modification*. Initially, these principles were used in the psychiatric hospitals, mental retardation institutions, and in the elementary and secondary school settings. It was not until the 1970s that Skinner's operant conditioning (i.e., OBM) was considered as a viable alternative to managing employee behavior. Even at present, opponents criticize these principles of operant conditioning and behavior modification from the standpoint that we are trying to control or regulate an individual's behavior without their knowledge or permission. On the other hand, the vast majority of human rewards and punishments are very common and present in our conceptions of a normalized environment (Hilgard and Bower, 1966; Kreitner, 1982).

In the early 1960s, the first significant signs of the use of OBM was described in an article in the *Harvard Business Review*, "Of Pigeons and Men" (Aldis, 1961). Aldis proposed that varying schedules of reinforcement be used in industrial settings to improve the performance of workers. The 1960s were filled with controversy on the use of OBM. The classic case at Emery Air Freight was testimonial to the effective use of positive reinforcement. Following discouragement from the lack of success of sales-training programs, Edward Feeney began a new program which used programmed learning principles combined with feedback. Annual sales nearly tripled. Also, a dramatic improvement in customer service relations and shipping efficiency were demonstrated following the use of positive reinforcement (At Emery Air Freight, 1973). Frederiksen (1982) noted that OBM has experienced a significant increase in use in the past few years and that it had significant promise in the management of employee behavior in the future.

Operant (OBM) Techniques

As previously noted, the work of Pavlov, Watson, Tolman, Thorndike, and Skinner were basic to our current concepts of OBM. The general thrust of OBM is to reinforce appropriate behavior, punish or extinguish inappropriate behavior, and to shape or train new behaviors. Terminology specific to the concept of behavior modifications (operant conditioning) or OBM as it applies in the employee realm include several concepts (Hilgard and Bower, 1966; Kazdin, 1984; Kreitner, 1982), described below.

Positive Reinforcement. Based on Thorndike's Law of Effect, individuals tend to repeat those behaviors which are perceived to be rewarding (reinforcing). Reinforcement is not the same as reward. The manager's selection of a reinforcer may or may not be perceived by the employee as being rewarding. Use of an employee-needs analysis to determine those items which have reinforcing value may be required. Positive reinforcers can include money, praise, awards, preferred parking spaces, extra time off with pay, and other perks such as feedback.

Negative Reinforcement. The removal of an aversive stimulus or a negative consequence. For example, the supervisor stops reminding the employee of his/her tardiness in coming to work when the employee begins coming to work on time.

Extinction. The process by which one ignores a given behavior. Examples include ignoring an employee's off-color jokes, or an employee's requests for a salary increase. Extinction should not be used when significant dysfunctional behavior occurs, such as unauthorized absences from work. It also is related to positive reinforcement. In this respect, should a desired behavior fail to be continuously (or intermittently) reinforced, then the absence of a reinforcer will generally elicit extinction of the desired behavior. On the other hand, an "extinction burst" refers to a sudden, spontaneous increase in behavior following withdrawal of a reinforcer; it tends to be short-lived.

Punishment. The presentation or application of a consequence which the employee perceives to be undesirable or punishing. For example, docking an employee's pay for being late, demotion of the employee, or denial of an employee's request for time off would probably be considered punishing by most employees.

Shaping. The progressive rewarding of positive employee behaviors which increasingly resemble a target goal through "successive approximation." For example, each time the employee increases productivity a little more, partial reinforcement is given. The goal is to shape the behavior toward a terminal performance goal.

Modeling. The employee "models" or imitates the supervisor's, manager's, or a co-worker's behavior which is determined to be positive. The use of a mentor-protege relationship is an example of a positive modeling activity. The mentor will shape the employee protege's behavior through a series of rewards as the protege's behaviors become closer and closer to that of the model's.

Immediacy of Reinforcement or Punishment. For either a reinforcer or punisher to be the most effective, it should be presented as soon after the behavior as possible. Delay of reward or punishment is considerably less effective.

Schedules of Reinforcement. There are four common schedules of reinforcement. Each depends upon the type of behavior to be reinforced. *Fixed Interval*—a reinforcer is delivered following a fixed passage of time. Example: a weekly or monthly paycheck. Best used for those behaviors which are not contingent upon temporal or special performance criteria. *Variable Interval*—an inconsistent reinforcement schedule (VI:5 might denote that a reinforcer is delivered following an *average* of five minutes). Considered to be an intermittent form of reinforcement which has a high reinforcing value once a behavior has been learned. *Fixed Ratio*—commonly termed a "units-of-production" schedule. For example, an employee is paid following completion of fifty hours of patient counseling. Also is known as a "piece-rate" method of reinforcement. Best used when the individual is better suited (due, perhaps, to slow rate of behavior) for reinforcement following successful completion of a given number of tasks. Finally, the *Variable Ratio* schedule delivers reinforcement following an *average* number of completed behaviors. For example, playing a Las Vegas slot machine is based upon a variable-ratio reinforcement schedule. It tends to be a very powerful reinforcer once the behavior has been learned.

Continuous versus Intermittent Reinforcement. Generally, continuous reinforcement (following each correct response) is best for developing new behaviors. The lower the level at which the employee is functioning, the greater is the need for continuous reinforcement, since it is related to the notion of immediate gratification. On the other hand, intermittent reinforcement is most powerful from the standpoint of maintaining a present behavior. An example is when the supervisor gives a periodic or random compliment to an employee, or when employees work for an undetermined Christmas bonus.

Generally, OBM principles can be learned by almost anyone who is motivated to do so. They can be learned through formal college courses or through staff development activities. There is a paradigm called the ABC process. Here, the *antecedent* (A) condition refers to the antecedent or predisposing event or behavior which tends to elicit a *behavior* (B) which is in response to the antecedent condition. Third, the *consequence* (C) refers to the action taken by another person in response to the behavior (B). The consequence portion is when OBM reinforcers or punishers are applied. Christian and Hannah (1983) indicated that effective managers knew about and how to use the operant (ABC) model for the purpose of eliciting an appropriate quantity and quality of employee behavior. They suggested that management was lawful; it followed laws of human behavior.

Reinforcement and Feedback

Reinforcement and feedback provided by an involved manager are very important components of any OBM model and can either facilitate or reduce the effectiveness of the process. Employees have a need for and desire positive reinforcement for desirable behavior. Without reinforcing a behavior or providing feedback (positive or negative) and/or involving the employee, positive employee behaviors can gradually be extinguished. Or the employee will learn to feel that "If I just put in my 8 and don't rock the boat, then I'll be rated adequate and I'll keep my job." As any management expert will tell you, *feedback* is an important component of any satisfactory supervisor/employee interaction. *Involvement* here refers to the active participation of the supervisor/

manager and the employee in the employee's motivation and performance process.

Reinforcement. Judi Komaki at Purdue University asked participants at three professional forums to tell her why the workplace was often lacking in the use of reinforcement. About 51 percent of the approximately sixty forum participants indicated that cultural factors were the reason. Participants indicated that most of us grew up in an environment where reinforcement was not part of our culture; people are used to being controlled aversively. Some of the participants noted that they were embarrassed by positively reinforcing people in that it was not "macho." Another 15 percent of the participants listed personality factors as the reason for not reinforcing. These reasons included that the individuals felt it was too much trouble or they just didn't want to bother with reinforcing. About 12 percent reported that environmental factors—for example, they were too busy or performance standards were unclear—were reasons for not reinforcing. Finally, about 11 percent believed that positive reinforcement would be of little benefit and another 11 percent indicated that their employees rarely did anything worth recognizing (Komaki, 1983).

The findings reported by Komaki are depressing, but not surprising. I have rarely seen supervisors, managers, and administrators providing positive reinforcement for their employees' efforts. My experiences have revealed that most of these individuals incorporate *extinction* and *punishment* as their primary method of employee behavioral control. Most of these administrative personnel are generally too busy dealing with their own problems, hang-ups, shooting alligators, and managerial ambiguities for them to be truly aware of and responsive to their employee's behaviors. Most reinforcement appears to come from the employee's co-workers. During my college years, I worked at sundry hourly jobs, such as in restaurants, retail businesses, and some occasional part-time teaching. Rarely did I receive reinforcement (or punishment) for doing my work!

Daniels and Rosen (1984) stressed that the bottom line of managing employees' performance was to positively reinforce them for positive behavior. Feedback was also a critical issue. Performance management was considered to be an all-level activity, from top management down through the ranks. It was something you could not delegate! In a modern employment environment, managers must individualize their feedback to the employees; group pep talks were not seen as being very effective. The authors noted that most organizational problems relating to employees were those of motivation, that people needed positive reinforcement, and that a positive climate for employee accountability was the result of positive reinforcement. Fitts (1972) suggested that the use of systematic reinforcement could significantly increase an employee's feelings of self-concept (and perhaps morale). Considering a common problem among HSOs, absenteeism, Schmitz and Henemann (1980) cautiously indicated that there had been some evidence among ten studies which suggested that absenteeism could be reduced through the use of positive reinforcement programs. It was noted that further research was needed in this area.

Feedback. Prue (1981) said that performance feedback was the most widely used form of OBM in the organizational setting. According to Vinton (1987), feedback allowed employees to assess their performance accurately, learn from their errors, see how they were perceived by others, replace unproductive work habits, and examine alternate behaviors. Providing feedback to employees was noted to be a common problem among managers, and a number of managers are not trained in the proper use of feedback. Feedback or *knowledge of results* (Baker and Young, 1966; Thorndike, 1932) has been demonstrated to significantly increase performance accuracy. Learning of new material (behaviors) is aided following appropriate feedback to the individual; the behavior can be associated with the outcome (positive, it is to be hoped). Feedback also increases motivation.

The concept of *negative scanning* was suggested by Allen, Heatherington, and Lah (1986). In this scenario, positive feedback is not always provided when everything is going well. On the other hand, feedback may be negative, and this can cause passive resistance to innovation. A related concept is that of the *sandwich feedback.* Here, the supervisor sandwiches praise with punishment. Most employees recognize such techniques in spite of the supervisor's attempts at camouflage.

According to Lawler (1983), feedback is crucial since it enables the individual to have appropriate information with which to correct his or her behavior. We seem to have a need for a mirror or yardstick by which to gauge our behavior. Feedback also provides a component of intrinsic motivation to cue the individual to perform in an effective manner. As previously discussed, any system needs constant or periodic feedback so that it can be self-regulating and efficient.

Ilgen and Moore (1987), in discussing feedback, proposed that "when both quality and quantity are important performance criteria and are also inversely dependent, what constitutes 'specific and timely' feedback is uncertain" (p. 401). When high-quality and high quantity performance is needed, appropriate feedback should be used. Additionally, they noted that performance was best improved by providing specific feedback related to the task.

Incentives and Other Motivators

What may be motivating or reinforcing to one employee may not be so to another. Each individual has his or her own private repertoire of intrinsic and extrinsic motivators which prompt the person to strive toward optimal work achievement. Additionally, each organizational climate will determine which schema of productivity paradigms may work from the applied standpoint. As already noted, increased job satisfaction and morale do not necessarily lead to increased work productivity.

Historically, money was considered to be an important motivator. However, current practice has indicated that a variety of cognitive, social, material, and organizational items may be specifically motivating to a given individual. From a reductionist standpoint, one might say that every individual has his or her own price. This price may be intrinsic, extrinsic, or a combination of both.

In a pilot study, the author surveyed twenty-seven professional employees at one human service organization on eleven items related to employee productivity. On a dichotomous scale (Yes/No) the percent of respondents which believed the eleven items were motivating for productivity were: higher salary (56 percent), cash awards (22 percent), more feedback (52 percent), recognition (78 percent), more training (44 percent), time-off award (41 percent), better insurance benefits (7 percent), better supervision (30 percent), hiring better employees (37 percent), protected breaks (4 percent), and better promotional opportunities (50 percent). Respondents could mark several items, thereby resulting in percentages exceeding 100. The feedback item was marked 52 percent of the time as an item which might increase productivity. However, the need for recognition (78 percent) strongly suggested that the employee has a basic need to be recognized as an individual in the organization. These results were tentative and only suggested a possible trend in responding. In discussions with a number of human services employees in several facilities, this author believes that the lack of timely information across all three shifts accounts for a significant portion of the variance in morale, job satisfaction, and perhaps productivity. However, further research is continuing in this area.

In the area of incentive pay, Daniel C. Rowland at the Bank of America and Bob Greene at Reward Systems, Inc. indicated that organizations are under pressure to reduce overhead, and fixed-pay plans are being replaced with variable-pay plans in a number of organizations. These plans included bonus programs, commission plans, and group incentives (Rowland and Greene, 1987). Additionally, Dr. Thomas Rollins of Hay Management Consultants (Rollins, 1985) indicated that the pay-for-performance issue has been intensely examined. For example, by pairing a cash incentive with a task which was naturally attractive to an employee (intrinsic motivation) could diminish the individual's tendency to perform that task. Determining the rate of pay for a given level of performance was also perceived to be a difficult task, as employees may very well prefer the security of a regular paycheck with predictable promotions to the performance-based pay. On the other hand, highly productive employees might resent the customary automatic pay increases given to all regardless of performance. In sum, these writers indicated that the standard, automatic pay schedules are becoming obsolete. Over the past few years the concept of merit pay has been variously cussed and discussed among members of the educational community. It is this author's opinion that attempts at merit pay plans in the PRFs would be met with considerable opposition (Rollins, 1987).

Daniels and Rosen (1984) listed a number of possible items which employees might perceive as reinforcing. They included social, monetary, fringe, and other reinforcers. Specific ones were: letter of commendation, verbal praise, increased responsibility, choice of tasks, time off, secretarial service, training for better jobs, special assignments, job rotation, flexitime, parking spaces, gift certificates, and others. The reader is referred to their text for additional information. In regard to HSOs, Reid and Shoemaker (1984) indicated that feedback has been the most investigated staff management technique. Some forms have included public posting of performance, verbal praise or verbal feedback, and written private feedback. An important thing to remember is that reinforcers are specific to the individual. Often, a manager will think from his or her own perspective and reference point. To a professional earning $50,000 a year, a protected twenty-minute break may not be reinforcing, since professionals generally schedule their own time. On the other hand, an additional thirty minutes for lunch might be very reinforcing for a direct-service worker earning $12,000 a year.

We must identify reinforcers which are perceived by the recipient to be rewarding, not those rewarding to us.

MANAGING EMPLOYEE PRODUCTIVITY

Generally, I have said that motivation to produce can be either intrinsic within the individual or extrinsic to the individual. The greatest degree of motivation is that which comes from within the individual. External coercers can work for a time, but they are not continually effective and do not facilitate positive employee morale and satisfaction on the job.

There are two major issues in employee productivity management. The first is the management of *ineffective performance*; the second is the management of *positive performance*. To motivate (or encourage) an employee to produce his or her best is significantly more difficult than to terminate the employee for ineffective performance. Motivation and management theory aside, the manager or organization is dealing with unique individuals who must be dealt with on an individual basis if their ultimate productivity is to be realized.

Managing Ineffective Performance

Characteristically, ineffective performance has been dealt with through the OBM techniques of extinction and punishment. These are two very powerful, efficient tools; however, they do not necessarily promote good relations with the employee. Perhaps good relations are not crucial at this point. Miner and Brewer (1983) stressed that effective or ineffective performance was related to a control model of successful performance as defined by the organization. Since specific criteria are at times difficult to determine, ineffective performance was believed to be that which was *considered* to be ineffective by the organization. Typical performance criteria were noted to include quality and quantity of output, absenteeism, the impact of the performance upon other employees, organizational stress generated, and the presence of any dishonest behavior.

In business organizations, Miner (1963, 1966, 1975) discussed a variety of problem areas associated with ineffective performance. These included the employee's job knowledge, emotional state, basic motivation to work, physical condition, family situation, work group, company, and a variety of situational factors affecting the work setting. Steinmetz (1969) suggested that the lack of a motivating environment, incorrect job assignment and supervision, lack of training, laziness, personality conflicts, failure to understand one's job duties, absenteeism, substance abuse, sex, social values, and labor-management values could affect one's performance.

Corrective actions for ineffective employee performance have included threats and disciplinary actions, counseling, alcohol and drug control programs, training and development, and others. Threats and discipline were suggested as being appropriate when employee conduct or work standards were not valued by the employee. With substance abuse problems, punitive methods are not always effective. The Ford Motor Company established the first industry counseling program in 1914. Originally, it focused on employee personal problems rather than upon ineffective performance. This concept rapidly increased in the work setting over the years through the use of Employee Assistance Programs (EAPs). Many organizations are using substance abuse control programs in order to salvage otherwise good employees. Training programs have been used primarily to correct basic skill deficiencies as well as for upgrade and renewal training (Miner and Brewer, 1983).

The HSOs, especially the PRFs, have not always had the luxury of managing ineffective performance in a creative manner. Federal standards frequently mandate the type and number of employees which must be on duty for a given class, in relation to the issue of staff-to-patient ratios. Given a labor market area which does not readily provide an abundance of job applicants for a given position and class, the HSO may be forced to hire average or below-average individuals in order to comply with federal standards. Certain professional positions may go vacant for as long as twelve to eighteen months for lack of applicants. With direct-service positions, some individuals may be hired, fired (or they voluntarily quit), and rehired one or more times in a given year. Once the employee in a state merit system has tenure or "status" with the system, it often requires a proven case of patient abuse or a felony before the individual can be terminated. Then, the appeal process begins! It is not uncommon for the employee to remain on the payroll indefinitely, even past a characteristic twenty, twenty-five, or thirty year tenure to retirement even if the employee has displayed only average or even marginal productivity. I am aware of some instances where direct-service workers were found guilty of some patient abuse but were transferred to a non-patient area rather than being fired.

To further complicate the picture, supervisors may be either unable or unwilling to conduct required employee performance evaluations. This greatly reduces the employee's opportunity for formal feedback, and any poor performance may exceed the statute of limitations, so to speak. While the subject of supervisor bias in performance evaluation is outside of the scope here, suffice it to say that supervisors have been known to rate an employee average or below to prevent another supervisor from recruiting the employee. Additionally, some supervisors may fail to evaluate an employee due to personality issues, such as not wanting to give good (or bad) news. I have known several supervisors and managers who were so disorganized and non-detail-oriented that they were unable (or unwilling) to get their act together for the detail of a performance evaluation. Perhaps such supervisors should have their paychecks withheld until they do their required evaluations?

A number of state personnel systems incorporate range and step systems of pay. Ranges are determined by an evaluation of knowledges, skills, and abilities while steps are generally determined by entry, tenure, and promotional decisions. Most systems have a one-step salary increase following the employee's successful completion of the initial probationary period. Then, depending upon the employee's entry salary, it could be a year or two before the next increase. After the second increase, employees may have to wait two or more years before they are eligible for a length-of-service increase. The process can be saved, however, with an across-the-board salary adjustment based upon labor market pay scales. Here is a significant dilemma. After the employee receives the first increase, following the probationary period, there is no real monetary incentive to excel. The cost-of-living index continues to rise while salaries remain constant. This fact in itself becomes a punishing consequence, since the employee really receives a salary decrease each year due to the increase in the cost of living. Other perks are needed to offset this dilemma.

Managing Effective Performance

An increase in productivity can benefit both the individual and the organization, but there must be a system which allows the delivery of positive reinforcement for acceptable behavior. Granted, system punishers are needed to manage certain types of ineffective performance, such as absenteeism, insurbordination, patient abuse, and other HSO crimes. Back to the concept of equity in work, the employee must perceive that his or her effort will be rewarded; otherwise, extra effort may not be valued by the employee. Some employees are clinically motivated by an altruistic philosophy; however, I suspect that the vast majority of us are motivated by doing something worthwhile with our time and receiving money so that we can pay our bills and have a few niceties in life. If money were not a factor, people would not change jobs for more money, or all of us would volunteer our services to a cause.

Given the condition that all employees were equally motivated to produce the greatest amount of the best products or services for their salaries, we would not have any productivity problems in either the public or private sector. Unfortunately, this premise is a myth rather than a reality. Productivity begins with the individual and is stimulated by management philosophy, expectancies, and contingencies. It is currently being perceived that American workers (especially those of the baby-boom generation) do not have the historic American work ethic. Employees seem to have a "what's in it for me?" rather than a "what can I do for you?" modus operandi. A number of years past, I worked with a colleague who manipulated his work schedule so that he came to work only about 80 percent of the time. The rationale was that the HSO was only paying him about 80 percent of what he was worth! I have seen direct-service workers who stood around and appeared to be busy due to either a lack of job knowledge or a basic dislike for work (especially unpleasant tasks). This wouldn't have been a problem except that their supervisors were continually hidden away somewhere in the bowels of the facility.

A number of OBM writers (e.g., Hopkins and Sears, 1982) have stressed that in order to manage employee behavior one must first determine the nature of the performance expectations and second obtain a performance baseline by which to compare future performance. Next, performance goals and standards must be determined as criteria for acceptable performance. Third, job reassignment and training do not always facilitate an increase in productivity. Feedback has been noted to be a very important component of performance management and improvement. We all want to know how we stand—on the job and in life. The feedback can be either private or public. The use of either reinforcement or punishment (as the situation indicates) in conjunction with feedback has been shown to have a generally good effect upon performance. The use of positive reinforcers, regardless of how seemingly insignificant, has very good effects. Even a simple "Good job,

Frank!" or an appropriate pat on the back has worked wonders with employees. The use of HSO-sponsored cookouts, parties, and other activities works well.

We repeatedly see newspaper mentions and announcements of good employee performance in the private-sector business climate. However, we rarely see such public reinforcement with the HSOs. I am not sure why, but I have some private opinion on this one.

A *nine-step model* for productivity improvement was described by Hopkins and Sears (1982). Some of the high points included developing a baseline of the employee's performance, identifying areas for possible improvement, and assessing one's current management methods which impact upon the employee. It was also stressed that the use of a graphic feedback system was very effective to communicate performance results. Determining an estimate of the cost-benefit payoff of improved performance was also noted to be very important. This is closely related to the notions of utility as discussed in earlier chapters. The method needs to be installed and evaluated periodically to determine its effectiveness. Any successful productivity improvement program should be maintained and reused as well as improved upon over time.

The improvement of productivity in HSO settings was discussed by Riley and Frederiksen (1984). They noted that the use of OBM was not a panacea or quickfix for many problems associated with human services. It was stressed that OBM was a systematic and well-documented approach. They noted that one of the problems associated with OBM in HSOs was the difficulty of determining appropriate inputs and outputs in the service delivery system. It was suggested that employee behaviors must be targeted in specific terms so that change could be effected and measured. Finally, the authors noted that HSOs did not always have clear goals and objectives and that measurement of the bottomline could be difficult.

TOWARD INCREASED PRODUCTIVITY

A variety of issues have been discussed thus far, including the principles of OBM. It appears relatively safe to say that in either business and industry settings or the HSOs, there does not exist a panacea to increase employee motivation and productivity. On the other hand, the degree to which the employee possesses relevant competencies and the degree to which these competencies fit into the schema of the HSOs business will largely determine the employee's predisposition toward ultimate productivity. While all levels of employees probably function better within a climate of mutual acceptance and feedback, several concepts seem to be relevant to improving productivity.

Managers should attempt to communicate performance standards and expectancies while being consistent in their expectations. They should also be aware of their personal biases in terms of expectancies. People need to know where they stand in their job, and this is where feedback plays an important role. Praise should be given for positive performance, along with other forms of reinforcement perceived by the employee as being rewarding. Employees need to be kept informed of organizational happenings; this includes keeping the late-night, third shift informed—sometimes they are the last to know, and rumors ferment here.

Additionally, the manager should care sincerely about his or her employees. People are individuals, not androids destined to perform robotic work. They are also part of the organizational climate, and the means by which you accomplish your overall objectives. Assist subordinates when needed; stay away as appropriate. Close monitoring of professionals will only elicit resentment toward the supervisor. Defend your employees to the system when needed; don't make the employee feel he or she is out there alone. Attempt to create a sense of independence in employees; let them take responsibility for special projects as they desire.

Use common sense, good judgment, tact, and consideration when dealing with the employee. Treat the employee as an adult and deliver praise in public as appropriate. Recognize your employees for their accomplishments, privately or publicly. Allow the employees room to succeed or to fail; don't crowd them. Delegate as much as possible; however, don't assign all of the dirty, mundane jobs to your subordinates.

Provide management support for all employee levels, in the form of appropriate performance appraisals and reviews. Assist the employees with materials, supplies, equipment, and other resources so they can actualize their jobs. Expect and insist upon good attendance by all employees. To allow absenteeism by some, without dealing with it, will only encourage feelings of resentment from others who have to work overtime or double shifts.

Be available to your employees without encouraging excessive dependence upon you. Time and time again I have heard direct-service workers complain that their supervisor was never around when needed.

Make serious attempts to run your department or service area in an efficient manner. Failure to respond to others' requests, sitting on paperwork, talking but not doing, procrastinating, and other dysfunctional behaviors will serve no useful and productive purpose. Don't let the "bureaucracy" of the bureaucracy bog down your employees, your department, or the system. Attempt to manage employees and your department in a pragmatic, cost-effective, resourceful manner. Develop an attitude in yourself and inculcate it into your employees that "I can," or "I will," rather than "These things take time," or "We must go through channels."

Eliminate the tendency to use a memo to communicate everything. Use the telephone and talk to people one-to-one. Be visible and supportive with your staff. Elicit the help of your subordinates in the decision-making process, seek their input, and thank them for their ideas. Don't turn a positive idea into a punishing experience by "rewarding" an employee with another project to do in exchange for doing a good job on the last one—unless, of course, the employee enjoyed the previous project. Keep communication lines open, get out of your office, get involved cognitively and behaviorally. If you seek information from others, use it, and give them feedback. Nothing demotivates like requiring others to submit a continual stream of information for your files and never giving them feedback. No one enjoys filling a "black hole" with information, especially if the information gathering process was not perceived as relevant in the first place.

We need to stop making excuses for our behavior, our inefficiency, and our problems with the system. We need to be action-oriented, believe in and respect others, and strive to accomplish our organizational goals together. After all, if we are experiencing a continual hassle with co-workers and our job, then the patients will undoubtedly feel this conflict and as a result their therapeutic progress will be impaired.

9

EMPLOYEE TRAINING AND PRODUCTIVITY

For an employee in any public- or private-sector organization to be productive the employee must initially have the requisite skills with which to perform the assigned job. Generally, the role of an employer is not that of a school. On the other hand, employers have traditionally engaged in on-the-job-training (OJT) activities by which to better prepare their new hires and tenured employees for current and changing roles. Since the post–World War II period in the United States there has been a cyclic process of generalization and specialization of workers. This variation has been very prevalent since the 1960s. Probably in excess of 90 percent of all businesses and organizations engage in some form of employee orientation or training. Billions of dollars are spent each year for training in the United States.

The mode of business and industry training formats for line employees has been typically that of a vocational nature. Wehrenberg (1987) noted that "OJT usually consists of a line supervisor showing an employee what to do, and how to do it, to produce some specific output or perform a specific step in a process" (p. 48). This format has generally been the essence of professional clinical training and direct-service worker training in personal care and habilitative skills.

TRAINING AND THE WORKPLACE

In the words of Michelangelo, "I am still learning." Training and education have similarities as well as differences. Generally, one thinks of *education* as that knowledge which one obtains through a process of formal study at the elementary, secondary, or post-secondary level. Education seeks to prepare one to deal with life and to formally indoctrinate one to recognize and process purposive, creative, and logical abstractions so that they may be used to solve problems. For the greatest part, the workplace is not in the business of educating its employees in that sense of the word.

Conversely, *training* is considered to be that process by which the individual is indoctrinated into the system, and is matured in the organization to perform an organizationally specific role which fosters a symbiosis of the employee and the employer. Hinrichs (1983) defined the notion of training as: "any organizationally initiated procedures which are intended to foster learning among organizational members" (p. 832). Landy and Trumbo (1980) suggested that training differed from general education in that the former was more specific and more practical to the work area. Furthermore, it was noted that efficient training involved efficiency by the learner, retention of the material learned, and transfer of training to the job setting. According to Landy (1985), training was considered to be a set of planned activities by which the organization was able to modify job knowledge and skills, and there must be an appropriate interface if training is to be functional and productive. Finally, the primary goal of training is to modify the employee's behavior in the work setting.

As the work environment continues to place heavy demands upon systems and the individual worker, both the individual employee and the organization have an obligation to prepare and maintain the employee at an optimal level of productivity and efficiency. An inefficient employee is a costly employee. In the business and industry sector, inefficient employees can make the difference between profit and loss. In the HSO environment, unqualified, poorly trained, and otherwise non-productive employees can thwart the therapeutic progress of a patient as well as place the organization in jeopardy from a human rights and federal funding standpoint. Inefficient and untrained employees put the patient at risk. On a lesser consequence, these behaviors hinder innovation and progress in treatment models.

Following the earlier era of the Harvard Business School's rational management model, American business has been vacillating between the rigid notions of the rational MBA graduate and those of the graduate who is more of a generalist and ultimately more adaptable. However, these issues are yet to be resolved and will probably never be. Presently, the HSO environment is significantly involved in specialist training and recruitment. A potentially good and dependable employee who wants to work in human services is out of luck unless the individual wishes to enter as a direct-service aide or possesses one of scores of specialty certifications, licensures, or other shingle entitlement.

No longer is a person with a master's degree or doctorate in a non-clinical track of psychology able to find a viable position in one of the more prestigious HSO environments. In particular, unless one has participated in a clinical psychology program approved by the American Psychological Association (APA), with requisite pre- and post-doctoral internships, the practice of most clinical psychology areas is off limits. States increasingly require master's-level individuals to have specialty licensure for work in community mental health centers and mental retardation facilities. Generic direct-service-worker positions are increasingly designated as entry-level, requiring special OJT activities and inservice classes within a year or so if the individual is to remain employed. We are in an era of Licensed Mental Health Technicians (LMHTs), Certified Medication Aides (CMAs), Developmental Training Specialists (DTSs), Licensed Nursing Home Administrators (LNHAs), Certified Alcoholism Counselors (CACs), and a myriad of other alphabetical specialties over and above the traditional licensed professional occupations. The 1980s has been an era of increased licensure awareness and specialization in our HSOs.

As Naisbitt (1984) noted, we are actively in the *Information Age*, which includes a strong movement toward decentralization of culture and function. We are becoming increasingly more oriented toward high technology and specialization. Information is increasing at enormous rates and as a result one must specialize if one is to achieve an appropriate niche in the workplace. We are obsessed with specialization. For example, try to "Have it Your Way" at McDonald's! You can, but you have to wait for a special order. There is the implication that specialization goes hand-in-hand with efficiency and profitability.

In their poignant book, *The Work Revolution*, Schwartz and Neikirk (1983) noted that the work environment is having to adapt to a changing work force. The baby-boomers are approaching or are at middle-age now. We are losing our youth population and are adding to our older population. There will be an increase in the number of "smart jobs" which require more education and training and creative thinking just to compete. It was noted that there were insufficient well-qualified attendants in mental hospitals or guards in prisons. As the result of significant trends in job restructuring and worker displacement, there will be additional needs for retraining the work force to perform new and more specific jobs in an attempt to thwart skill obsolescence.

Current employee jobs are continually being upgraded. We are well aware of the impact of microcomputers upon traditional typewriter usage. This obviously creates a vast need for clerical and secretarial retraining. Schwartz and Neikirk indicated that in 1983 the expenditures for education and job training in the United States were about $210 billion, which translated to about $930 for a per capita expenditure. Another thrust is the federal Job Training Partnership Act (JTPA), which set up a process by which communities could become involved in the retraining of Americans through Private Industry Councils (PICs). The PICs coordinate training incentives and other activities through private business enterprise.

Due to increased worker specialization, automation, and high technology, more and more workers will become what Schwartz and Neikirk termed *structurally unemployed.* As such, fewer workers will be needed to produce more work. On the other side (as in human service organizations), new and changing skill demands will create skill deficits or obsolescence for existing workers, while continuing federal mandates have been increasing the need for HSO workers. The concept of *frictional unemployment* refers to the inability to match applicants with job openings. In our HSOs, we have seen these trends with a number of specialties such as recruiting adequate numbers of qualified registered nurses, and others such as occupational therapists, speech pathologists, and physical therapists. In fact, employers are paying special bonuses to individuals in low-supply professions—which is setting the stage for issues in pay inequity for other professions. The individual with a generic human services degree or orientation is becoming passé, except perhaps in the administrative ranks.

TRAINING AND PRODUCTIVITY

According to Schmidt, Hunter, and Pearlman (1982), an organization's overall success depends both upon the selection and placement of quality new hires and upon the degree to which the employee is effectively managed after being hired. The more productive the employee can become, the greater the organization's return on its investment will be. It was estimated that the typical worker produced about twice his or her annual salary. Since it was noted that good employee selection programs had high validity and a low selection ratio, selection of quality employees would reduce, though not eliminate, the need for additional training. The process of utility analysis (Cascio, 1982) can assist in determining the cost-effectiveness of such training.

Training was noted to represent an investment in human capital by

Paul C. Ross of American Telephone and Telegraph Company (Ross, 1982). Any such training program should be approached from a business standpoint. It was suggested that if an organization increased its expenditures on training by about 50 percent using state-of-the-art methods, there could be a greater than 400 percent improvement in training efficiency. Finally, it was emphasized that training activities should be viewed as an investment in employee resources, not a cost per se.

At Hewlett-Packard in Cupertino, California, Lee (1984) reported that nine full-time trainers assisted by eighty-five other support personnel provided about 28,980 training hours for some 3,649 employees in 1983. The $1.7 million training budget included about 61 percent of expenditures for off-site meetings. Training was perceived to be a critical area in the company and was considered to be a profit-center rather than a cost item. Needs analyses as well as training validation were integral parts of the system. In another study, of about 300 executives in Fortune 500 firms, Craig (1984) reported on an externally contracted study which revealed that about 94 percent of the firms were involved in some form of employee retraining. Vocational schools, two-year colleges, universities, and other institutions were used to provide this training. In sum, these business and industry studies have evidenced considerable responsiveness to employee training in the private sector.

The international accounting firm Arthur Andersen Company has an elaborate facility west of Chicago. Their commitment to training is evidenced by their state-of-the-art training facility—an ex-college campus which employs over 300 master's- and doctoral-level personnel. Another familiar training facility is that of Mountain Bell Telephone in Denver. They too have a rather extensive employee training center, which includes vocational, technical, and professional programs. Other progressive facilities include McDonald's, Burger King, IBM, and Hewlett-Packard, to name only a few. The common theme in each of these progressive training programs is that of commitment to training excellence combined with appropriate funding for their programs. The HSOs could learn some lessons.

Some training opponents have indicated that due to a variety of employee and organizational variables and employee motivations, some training situations do not always produce performance improvements. On the other hand, there is adequate documentation in the management and training literature that training is beneficial and can promote improvement in employee efficiency and productivity. In a critical review of several articles, Ziarnik and Bernstein (1982) addressed the scope of training in PRFs serving the mentally retarded. They concluded that prior to about the mid–1960s, only about 5 percent of fifty-five surveyed institutions had training programs. But, they noted, between about 1972 and 1982 there was a significant increase in the number of facilities having training programs. Most of this increase appeared to have been due to the shift from custodial to active habilitation models of treatment. Some of the problems with such training programs were noted to be due to poor design and implementation. The reviewers also suggested that if the environmental climate facilitated poor employee performance, then training would not solve the problems. It was perceived that the identification of goals and training outcomes was crucial if a maximization of training dollars was to be realized. The reader is referred to Ziarnik and Bernstein for further insight.

TRAINING-NEEDS ASSESSMENT

Any form of training requires some effort to determine training needs. Essentially, if there is no need for a particular training component, then the training should not occur. Goldstein (1986) stressed that if one's training was to be systematic, then needs assessment, development and implementation of the training program, followed by evaluation and continual modification (feedback looping in the system), should occur. We are generally cognizant that some organizations and/or managers are not always receptive to the training process. Some may merely continue to hire and fire employees until a satisfactory one is found. Others may only pay lip service to training and provide minimal resources for the training section or department. Still others may advocate training, but somehow fail to encourage the development and maintenance of a quality, efficient, and relevant training program. Finally, others may periodically change the administrative directives so that training programs continually undulate in a state of disorganization and misdirection. Ford and Noe (1987) noted that "Managers with negative attitudes toward training may report less need for training than do managers with positive attitudes towards training" (p. 50).

Among 901 respondents (50 percent return rate) of a West Virginia survey of hospital and community mental health personnel, Ellis and Linton (1982) reported that non-credentialed personnel, especially state hospital psychiatric aides, were probably the individuals most in need of training. It was suggested that skill-oriented training at the actual work setting was probably the most relevant for such personnel. In regard to employee professionalism, Christian and Hannah (1983) noted that when HSO personnel were provided with training in a professional format, then this modeling would encourage the employees to perform in a professional manner.

Specific training needs for almost any organization or business include a continuum from new-employee orientation to preretirement preparation. Some general categories of training include company orientation, departmental orientation, work area orientation, special OJT training, supervisory training, managerial training, performance deficit training, continuing education credits for maintaining one's license, and promotional training. Training may also be indicated following an employee's performance review which revealed certain performance deficits. Each of these training areas encompasses different criteria for trainee selection and instructional format.

Hinrichs (1983) emphasized that in the systems approach to employee training, training activities encompassed the individual, the training program itself, and finally the total organization. Additionally, needs analysis, training inputs and outputs, feedback, and evaluation were crucial components of any training activity or system.

Increasing the employee's level of self-awareness, skills, and motivation to perform a job were additional purposes of training, according to Wexley and Latham (1981). They stressed that training programs sought to better equip the employee to solve job-related problems as well as to better prepare the employee for productive decision-making.

TRAINING IN HUMAN SERVICE ORGANIZATIONS

Every new hire entering the culture of an organization should have appropriate pre-service orientation if the individual is to feel part of the organizational culture. Without proper and thorough orientation, the new hire will become a victim of confusion, uncertainty of function, and estrangement. Essentially every HSO provides new-hire orientation—but if the process is haphazard and incomplete, then the employee and the system will be handicapped.

In the PRFs, there is often a crunch to maintain adequate staffing ratios by which to comply with federal standards with the result that the patient is served better. When the PRF is located in a rural area in a small community setting, the labor market supply can easily be exhausted. Thus, certain employees may be recycled through the system over a period of time, including some who had been terminated earlier for less than desirable performance. Given the large numbers of direct-service workers needed, community resources may very well be inadequate to supply previously trained and experienced new hires. For direct-service-worker employees, training needs are the greatest.

In about the mid–1970s, King (1976) indicated that the health care industry was rapidly becoming the second largest industry in the United States. In the 1980s this has been very evident with a significant change in the nature of health care services. In particular, a variety of health maintenance organizations have been in operation. We are also experiencing a new thrust in care for the aged as well as in the continued deinstitutionalization of our PRFs. Due to the significant degree of individualized patient care services being required in our hospitals for proper patient care, King (1976) noted that the movement away from the 200-year history of physician-dominated medical care was causing a revolution in these services. With this change, new skills and jobs are becoming needed to fill this patient-care gap.

Training in a health care facility may be a function of the personnel department and separate from the nursing education function (King, 1976). More currently, an organization's human resources department may incorporate all training functions, but not always. Traditionally, nursing departments have, to a certain degree, controlled patient-care-related training. Personnel departments have been responsible for new-employee orientation and sundry activities such as management training. There is also the general notion that training should be conducted by an individual knowledgeable in the job specialty area. This is often facilitated by standards of competence established by state boards of nursing, medicine, and other specialty practices. Competency-based training has been the standard.

The current concepts of centralized versus decentralized professional departments have caused additional training problems. With a centralized departmental system, training can be handled more expeditiously and perhaps more standardized. On the other hand, when professional service practitioners are decentralized into unit management systems, the training process can break down if it is not orchestrated by a centralized training department. The industry practice of employee orientation and coaching by work station and departmental supervisors also occurs in the HSOs. However, if these training supervisors are not cognizant of efficient ways by which to conduct adult training, then the training effects can be haphazard if not grossly inefficient. The notion that someone who has skill expertise can also train others effectively is somewhat naive. True, some expert practitioners can in fact train well. Others cannot. If one has technical skill but lacks training skill, then the potential trainer must be trained for the training role.

Despite of our state of knowledge in learning theory, effective training methods, instructional design, use of instructional media, and other issues, our HSOs do not always have either the knowledge or the funds with which to develop and implement a viable training program. Even supervisory training programs conducted by state offices which train "by the numbers" are not always appropriate or effective. It is not uncommon for trainers (or academicians, for that matter) to go through the motions of training being either unprepared or unmotivated to develop state-of-the-art training regimes. Of course, funding resources can preclude some activities.

This writer recalls some not-too-great examples of HSO training programs. In one PRF, the training department was composed of one ex-teacher, an ex-minister, and two near-retirement old-timers. The training thrust was primarily toward new-employee orientation, first aid, cardiopulmonary resuscitation, and a version of behavioral intervention techniques. Professional training was nil for the most part. In another facility, new-employee orientation was it; professionals competed for funds to attend external workshops and conferences. In still another PRF, the training director was hired to work with the nursing director. Due to some conflicts and organizational priorities and restructuring, the training operation continued to be in a state of turmoil for months. In each of these settings, professional trainers were not present, and organizational philosophy or politics precluded a progressive training program from developing.

Even when first-line supervisors conduct employee training, such training models, media, and formats should be developed by competent and experienced instructional designers and developers. In this respect the American Society for Training and Development produced an extensive role and competency model for trainers. This plan can serve as one guideline for developing effective training personnel (ASTD, 1983). There is also a notion that teachers will make good trainers. Unfortunately, this is not always true. Classically, teachers may not always be cost-oriented and criterion-referenced in their training methods. In the business, industry, and organizational setting, training models should always be focused upon job-related, criterion-referenced instruction. There is the idea that one should teach the employee what is needed to perform one's job better and more efficiently without going overboard on theory and peripheral information.

Next to improved employee performance, the other major goal of in-service training is for the employee to be able to transfer (generalize) this training to the actual work environment. Training must be applied for it to be relevant and successful. Wexley and Latham (1981) provided several suggestions for training retention and generalization. The training and job setting must interface. In this respect, what is imparted in the training must have relevance for the work to be done. The learned material must be practiced, because practice facilitates positive transfer. Use of a variety of example and training techniques will also encourage transfer. For one to train solely by lecture will reduce effectiveness. The significant aspects of the task to be trained for must be identified so that any step-by-step procedures are clear in the trainee's mind. Practice and understanding of the principles that are the focus of the family are necessary prior to effective transfer taking place. For training to increase motivation and improved performance, the immediate supervisor should provide rewards to the employee for improved performance. Trainees must be able to identify the relevance and applicability of any training. Finally the authors suggested that the use of relevant, thought-provoking questions would encourage transfer.

Training authorities all stress the use of training-needs assessments, relevance of instructional content, use of positive reinforcement, provision for feedback, and the development and maintenance of a system by which the training effects can be evaluated (Craig, 1976; Hinrichs, 1983; King, 1976; Landy, 1985; Landy and Trumbo, 1980; and Wexley and Latham, 1981). Training must be designed, developed, implemented, and evaluated in a systems framework with criterion-referencing of instructional content being emphasized.

ADULT LEARNING MODEL

There is said to be an old Arabian proverb which states that "An old camel will still carry the load of many young asses." Similarly, the adult learner, termed the *non-traditional student*, is a rich resource of competencies. As such, the adult student does not learn well through a traditional model of "read, remember, regurgitate." The adult student brings to the training setting a rich resource of life experiences, learning styles, curiosities, and motivations not always found in the traditional secondary or post-secondary vocational educational or college student. The adult learner needs to interact with his or her peers in the classroom or training setting (as well as with the instructor or trainer) and needs to be able to relate the relevance of the training to the work setting *now*. The adult learner learns because of a *need to know* or a *need to achieve* and not because someone is coercing him or her to attend school. Although, in some instances, the organization may very well "volunteer" the adult employee to attend a class or training program, in the end, the employee wins with increased knowledges, skills, abilities, and a richer repertoire of positive interpersonal relationship skills.

The German poet and philosopher Goethe once remarked that "There is nothing more terrifying than ignorance in action." Undoubtedly, this applies to the adult worker who fails to keep updated in his or her trade or profession. Plato was reported to have said that "Man . . . is the most savage of all the products of the earth if he is inadequately and improperly trained." Morgan, Holmes, and Bundy (1976) noted that an individual will be employed in up to ten different occupations during his or her lifetime and that new skill acquisition was inherent in such change. They also stressed that an individual with a formal education was more prone to maintain the education than one who has little education.

Morgan et al. further indicated that the adult learner has a strong desire to learn and the instructional climate should be informal, with adequate opportunity for participation and interaction. Adult education involves and takes advantage of the adults' superior ability to solve problems and to plan since they have a rich repertoire of experience. Instructional materials should be on the adult's level of understanding and relevant to the job. Behavioral or performance objectives should be defined, and the trainer should follow them. The adult is an active learner and is generally high motivated. A variety of instructional techniques is desirable. For a rather detailed discussion of the adult learning model, as well as of training in general, the reader should consult Craig (1976) and Morgan et al. (1976) for comprehensive procedures and techniques.

10

RECRUITING FOR EXCELLENCE: FACT OR FALLACY?

This book has presented a variety of issues related to motivation and productivity in human service organizations. The continual dilemma of the HSO bureaucracy, traditions, organizational climate and cultures, and the various internal human issues such as turfism can be problematic for optimal employee productivity. Barriers to motivation and productivity can be numerous and monumental. Human factors such as the people/jobs fit, stress, and employee problems often prevail. While theory and practice do not always equate and do not appear to offer a panacea for increasing employee motivation and productivity, the area of organizational behavior management has continued to appear promising in both the private and public sectors. Finally, training appears to be a critical issue with the HSO employee, both for new hires and tenured employees. But, given these issues, how does one recruit for excellence? Can it be done? Is it feasible? This writer believes the HSO can obtain new quality employees as well as improve the skills of existing good employees.

ORGANIZATIONAL NEEDS AND CHANGING AGENDAS

Historically, our general hospitals have administered to the physically ill, with creative medicine being only a dream. Our PRFs for the mentally ill and the mentally retarded have goals of containment and order. The prisons have had goals of removal from society. Nursing homes have served the medically terminal and psychologically demented. Community-based partial care facilities and halfway houses were slow to emerge. When one went to a hospital, one was glad to get better; if one died, that was fate. Now, patients *expect* to get better, and if there is a medical error then the patient sues the practitioner, with the juries awarding outrageous malpractice sums. In the psychiatric and mental retardation facilities, federal mandates under Title XIX and other regulations dictate how treatment is to occur. Certification or decertification is a major issue. Even the Department of Justice is investigating HSO facilities regarding the issue of patient rights. Is there any end in sight? Has litigation become the essence of medical and psychiatric practice, or are we currently dealing with an overly neurotic, litigious society?

Standards are increasing in complexity and in the degree of specificity for compliance. Federal survey teams have been said to have an agenda-of-the-month. That is, the regulations are so obscure in some areas that the federal teams might arbitrarily pick a category of standards (such as nursing care plans) to investigate on a facility site visit. Survey teams themselves fail to agree on regulations and on whether or not a facility is in compliance.

Given the political environment of our HSOs, especially the PRFs, perhaps some administrators do not become too excited about motivation and productivity issues. They are too busy putting out fires and shooting alligators. Since the 1960s there has been a continual movement, with varying highs and lows, toward deinstitutionalization of patients. On the other hand, our community resources continue to be grossly inadequate, understaffed, undertrained, and underfunded. Opponents of the institutions say they are too expensive to operate due to declining patient censuses. Others have indicated that community-based facilities are not much cheaper to operate, due to the need to contract for specialized services and the lack of economy of scale. Training often is directed only at the correction of deficiencies. One facility receives a demerit for not having all employees trained in CPR. Then, a mass training effort is undertaken to get all employees trained in CPR.

Employee tenure at PRFs tends to be almost tri-modal. First, there is the group who do not remain there for even a year—in some cases, less than three months. Then there is the upwardly mobile group, who will probably move on within two to five years. Finally, there is the foundation of the organization, the long-tenured direct-service or managerial employees who have established roots in the community. Turnover among direct-service workers can easily exceed 50, 75, or even 100 percent at PRFs. High-demand professions, such as nursing, continue to be hard-pressed for sufficient employees. Some facilities have to "rent a nurse" in order to obtain coverage, often at significantly inflated hourly rates. On the other hand, the better funded, better managed, and more prestigious facilities tend to keep their employees longer than the generic facilities do.

In the midst of bureaucratic process, outdated physical facilities, high stress levels, and working with severe and chronic patients, the PRFs have definite handicaps in attracting and maintaining quality employees. The general hospitals and the more prestigious private mental retardation and psychiatric facilities have a better chance at recruitment, but even some of them are involved in active and aggressive recruiting campaigns. For example, a registered nurse can pick his or her location and can often specify a salary; it is a seller's market. Additionally, federal standards and state licensure boards are increasingly requiring better credentialed and licensed personnel to fill positions at the PRFs. Resultantly, additional recruiting burdens and funding problems occur.

COMPETING WITH BUSINESS AND INDUSTRY

For many of the HSO facility positions, there is no private-sector business and industry position equivalent. The ones which are equivalent would be found in the private psychiatric and specialized developmental disabilities organizations. On the other hand, larger private-sector business and industry firms recruit and employ registered nurses, occupational therapists, vocational instructors and counselors, psychologists, clerical and business office support personnel, and managerial staff. There is an indication, however, that a large number of individuals employed in HSOs prefer not to work in the business and industry sector. This may, in part, be due to personality issues, desires for bureaucratic security, and the lack of the hard-driving profit motive characteristic of the private sector.

The Schwartz and Neikirk (1983) notion of frictional unemployment as represented by the inability to match workers with available jobs appears to be relevant to HSOs. While the HSOs continually strive to be competitive in terms of salary levels, there are definite inequities associated with pleasing environments, promotional opportunities, and merit pay. Most public sector HSOs are structured on a range and step method of pay. This is an attempt to achieve pay equity for comparable job classes. However, the frequency with which promotions and step increases can occur is often fixed by state personnel policy. Unlike the profit-generating private sector, the public-sector environment must depend on state funding appropriations, and budgets tend to be fixed on an annual or bienniel basis, although there can be exceptions to the rule.

The primary issue in recruitment, hiring, and retention among HSOs is that of competition with similar facilities. While one does not necessarily recruit a registered nurse, physician, or psychologist from private industry, it can happen. Some potential HSO employees consider the PRFs to be the snake pit of the human services field. Other view this environment as a challenge, an opportunity to do research, and a valuable setting for experience in the hard-core human problem areas. In this respect, any number of universities place their master's and doctoral interns at such facilities for clinical training experiences. Then, unfortunately, most of these interns go to work for the better HSOs or enter private practice.

In order to compete with similar HSO facilities, a facility may have to reconsider and rethink its organizational climate, benefit package, salary schedule, and promotional opportunity structure. This writer has observed a variety of differences among HSO employers. For example, the general hospitals tend to have better working conditions, better benefit packages, and better salary schedules than do the PRFs. The PRFs will need to convince the state legislatures that additional funds are needed, better benefit packages are warranted, and facility discretionary funds (such as for training and equipment) are justified.

RECRUITING FOR EXCELLENCE

As the foundation for recruiting excellent employees the HSO needs to have a reputation itself for excellence. Yet there are excellent employees at the average or substandard facilities for a variety of reasons. People do not always have a choice as to their work setting or geographical location. Proactive organizational climates, competitive salary and benefit schedules, rational and understanding administrators, adequate program funding, aggressive public relations programs, modern physical plants, attractive facility grounds and landscaping, average or better perks for employees, recognition for good performance, and a high level of employee morale will do wonders for recruiting efforts. The word gets out. Given the employee's choice of a geographical location, a teaching and research climate, and good reputation, I dare say that the Menninger Foundation, Mayo Clinic, Johns Hopkins, and others don't have too much difficulty in finding and keeping quality employees. Of course, these are status institutions.

Some proponents of certification and licensure requirements have advocated the increase in licensure requirements for additional professions. For example, in Kansas, a new bill was passed by the legislature in 1987 to require that master's level psychologists be licensed at the master's level (doctoral licensure is reserved for private practice). A potential problem with this strategy is that many master's level psychological practitioners are employed at the state mental retardation institutions and community mental health centers. This may or may not affect future recruiting efforts.

Excellent employees can be found, but recruiting efforts must be aggressive, and benefits must be suitable for the potential employee. There must be flexibility in the state merit system and on the private HSO employer's side. Also, we may very well be in an era of increasing need for HSO practitioners and either a stable or decreasing supply of interested and qualified applicants. With direct-service, trades, maintenance, and other specialty positions some of the labor supply may very well be seasonal. It is known that some males hire on with institutions only when more macho jobs are in short supply. For the hourly employee, the HSO job may possibly be the best job available, considering the typical going wage and security of some private-sector job classes. With highly specialized positions such as physicians, dentists, pharmacists, and others, the salary schedule may be what you can hire the individual for. You have to pay what it takes to get the employee; the alternative is violation of federal standards of treatment and possible decertification.

THE FUTURE OF HUMAN SERVICES

The future is decentralization and specialization. We are moving from large, economy-of-scale facilities to community-based organizations. Health maintenance organizations are replacing traditional medical structures. The PRFs are increasingly being used for the most severely and chronically ill or incapacitated patient. We are having to provide for our increasing numbers of aged due to better health practices and other factors contributing to longer life. Given our large numbers of institutions in the United States, I do not foresee their significant elimination until after the year 2000. Even then, some will probably still be in operation. Our nursing care facilities are continuing to be under mandates for quality treatment.

Naisbitt (1984) indicated that in the future we will be moving more toward "self care," in areas such as fitness, wellness, stress control, hospice involvement, birthing alternatives (midwifery) and home-like birth delivery services, with a plethora of support groups. These predictions have been coming true at a rapid rate. Additionally, there may very well be a transition from hospital to home health care, with only the most serious cases being in traditional hospitals.

Non-dangerous criminal offenders are increasingly being used for public works activities. This is reminiscent of the many Works Progress Administration projects a number of years ago.

We are steadily finding more syndromes, diseases, and conditions which are neurochemically based. Since the 1950s and currently, significant strides are continuing in the chemical treatment of schizophrenia, manic-depressive illness, substance abuse, and senile dementia. In the 1960s we made great strides in the prevention of phenylketonuria (PKU), one cause of mental retardation. Currently, we are working on a cure for Alzheimer's disease, apparently with neurochemical implications. There are increasing ramifications of child and partner abuse, chemical dependency, stress, smoking, rape, irrational and violent crimes, and acquired immune deficiency syndrome (AIDS) which will be continuing areas of medical and psychiatric concern for years to come.

As Victor Hugo once said, "Time is the architect, the people the builder." We continue to discover new conditions and problems with humankind, yet it will be humankind that finds a solution.

REFERENCES

Abelson, M. A. (1987). Examination of avoidable and unavoidable turnover. *Journal of Applied Psychology, 72*(3), 382–386.

Adams, J. S. (1965). Inequity in social exchange. In L. Berkowitz (Ed.), *Advances in experimental social psychology* (Vol. 2), pp. 267–299. New York: Academic Press.

Adorno, T. W., Frenkel-Brunsurk, E., Lewinson, D. J., & Sandford, R. M. (1950). *The authoritarian personality.* New York: Harper.

Alderfer, C. P. (1969). An empirical test of a new history of human needs. *Organizational behavior and human performance, 4*, 142–175.

Alderfer, C. P. (1972). *Existence, relatedness, and growth: Human needs in organizational settings.* New York: The Free Press.

Aldis, O. (1961). Of pigeons and men. *Harvard Business Review*, July-August, 1961, 59–63.

Allen, G. J., Heatherington, L., & Lah, M. (1986). Human aspects of evaluation in institutional settings: Political, methodological, and social trade-offs. In J. Thaw & A. J. Cuvo (Eds.), *Developing responsive human resources* (pp. 261–302). Hillsdale, NJ: Erlbaum Associates.

ASTD. (1983). *Models for excellence: The conclusions and recommendations of the ASTD training and development competency study.* Washington, DC: American Society for Training and Development.

At Emery Air Freight (1973). At Emery Air Freight: Positive reinforcement boosts performance. *Organizational Dynamics, 1*, 41–50.

Atkinson, J. W. (1957). Motivational determinants of risk-taking behavior. *Psychological Review, 64*, 359–372.

Atkinson, J. W. (1964). *An introduction to motivation.* Princeton, NJ: Van Nostrand.

Atkinson, J. W. (1965). Some general implications of conceptual developments in the study of achievement oriented behavior. In M. R. Jones (Ed.), *Human motivation: A symposium.* Lincoln: University of Nebraska Press.

Baird, J. E. (1984). Improving productivity in health care through quality circles. In J. M. Virgo (Ed.). *Health care: An international perspective.* Edwardsville, IL: International Health Economics and Management at Southern Illinois University.

Baker, C. H., & Young, P. (1966). Feedback during training and retention of motor skills. *Canadian Journal of Psychology, 14*, 254–264.

Balk, W. L. (1975). Technological trends in productivity measurement. *Public Personnel Management, 4*, 128–133.

Bandura, A. (1969). *Principles of behavior modification.* New York: Holt, Rinehart, and Winston.

Bandura, A. (1978). The self system in reciprocal determinism. *American Psychologist, 33*, 344–358.

Beehr, T. A., & Franz, T. M. (1987). The current debate about the meaning of job stress. In J. M. Ivancevich and D. C. Ganster (Eds.), Job stress: From theory to suggestion (pp. 5–18); *Journal of Organizational Behavior Management, 8* (Whole No. 2).

Beehr, T. A., & Newman, J. E. (1978). Job stress, employee health, and organizational effectiveness: A facet analysis, model, and literature review. *Personnel Psychology, 31*, 665–699.

Berne, E. (1964). *Games people play.* New York: Grove.

Braceland, F. J. (1966). Rehabilitation. In S. Arieti (Ed.), *American handbook of psychiatry* (Vol. 3) (pp. 643–656). New York: Basic Books.

Brunsson, N. (1985). *The irrational organization.* Chichester, England: Wiley.

Buchanan, B. (1974). Building organizational commitment: The socialization of managers in work organizations. *Administrative Science Quarterly, 19*, 533–546.

Buffum, W. E., & Konick, A. (1982). Diagnosing job satisfaction in mental health institutions. (Research Report). Columbus, OH: Ohio State Department of Mental Health and Mental Retardation.

Bureau. (1974). Employee absenteeism and turnover. Washington, DC: Personnel Policies Forum, Bureau of National Affairs.

Bureau. (1985). *Statistical abstract of the United States.* (105th Ed.). Washington, DC: Bureau of the Census, U.S. Department of Commerce, United States Government Printing Office.

Campbell, J. P., & Pritchard, R. D. (1983). Motivation theory in industrial and organizational psychology. In M. D. Dunnette (Ed.), *Handbook of industrial and organizational psychology* (pp. 63–130). New York: Wiley.

Cannon, W. B. (1914). The interrelations of emotions as suggested by recent physiological researches. *American Journal of Psychology, 25*, 256–282.

Cannon, W. B. (1935). Stresses and strains of homeostasis. *American Journal of Medical Science, 189*, 1–14.

Cascio, W. F. (1982). *Applied psychology in personnel management* (2nd Ed.). Reston, VA: Reston.

Cavanagh, M. E. (1984). In search of motivation. *Personnel Journal, 63*(1), 76–82.

Chapanis, A. (1983). Engineering psychology. In M. D. Dunnette (Ed.), *Handbook of industrial and organizational psychology* (pp. 697–744). New York: Wiley.

Cheloha, R. S., & Farr, J. L. (1980). Absenteeism, job involvement, and job satisfaction in an organizational setting. *Journal of Applied Psychology, 65*, 467–473.

Christian, W. P., & Hannah, G. T. (1983). *Effective management in human services*. Englewood Cliffs, NJ: Prentice-Hall.

Clarke, H. E., & Summers, L. R. (Eds.). (1975). *The living Webster dictionary of the English language*. Chicago: The English Language Institute of America.

Conrod, R. (1955). Comparison of paced and unpaced performance at a packing task. *Occupational Psychology, 29*, 15–24.

Cooper, C. L., & Marshall, J. (1976). Occupational sources of stress: A review of the literature relating to coronary heart disease and mental ill health. *Journal of Occupational Psychology, 49*, 11–28.

Cope, J. G., Grossnickle, W. F., Covington, K. B., & Durham, T. W. (1987). Staff turnover as a function of performance in a public residential facility. *American Journal of Mental Deficiency, 92*(2), 151–154.

Coulter, P. B. (1979). Organizational effectiveness in the public sector: The example of municipal fire protection. *Administrative Science Quarterly, 24*, 65–81.

Cowie, R. A. (1985). Dana's five steps for improving people involvement. In Y. K. Shetty & V. M. Buehler (Eds.), *Productivity and quality through people* (pp. 59–67). Westport, CT: Quorum.

Craig, R. L. (Ed.). (1976). *Training and development handbook: A guide to human resource development* (2nd Ed.). New York: McGraw-Hill.

Craig, R. L. (Ed.). (1984). Who and how employers retrain. *National Report for Training and Development (ASTD), 10*,(7), 4.

Curtis, W. R. (1986). The deinstitutionalization story. *The Public Interest, 85*, 34–49.

Cuvo, A. J., & Thaw, J. (1986). Mental disability law—the politics of human rights. In J. Thaw & A. J. Cuvo (Eds.), *Developing responsive human resources* (pp. 191–228). Hillsdale, NJ: Erlbaum Associates.

Daft, R., & Becker, S. (1978). *Innovation in organizations*. New York: Elsevier.

Daniels, A. C., & Rosen, T. A. (1984). *Performance management: Improving quality and productivity through positive reinforcement* (2nd Ed., Rev.). Tucker, GA: Performance Management Publications.

Davis, C. K. (1984). Reforming the U.S. health care financing system. In J. M. Virgo (Ed.), *Health care: An international perspective*. Edwardsville, IL: International Health Economics and Management at Southern Illinois University.

Dawis, R. V., Loftquist, L. H., & Weiss, D. J. (1968). A theory of work adjustment: A revision. *Minnesota Studies in Vocational Rehabilitation, No. 23*. Minneapolis: University of Minnesota Press.

Descartes, R. (1649). Passions of the soul. In E. S. Haldane & G. R. T. Ross (Eds.), *Philosophical works of Descartes*. Cambridge: University Press, 1911. Reprinted by Dover, 1955.

Dickens, C. (1842). *American notes for general circulation* (Vol. I) (3rd Ed.) (pp. 105–111) London: Chapman and Hall.

Downs, A. (1968). *Inside bureaucracy*. Boston: Little, Brown.

Drucker, P. (1954). *The practice of management*. New York: Harper and Row.

Dunham, R. B., & Smith, F. J. (1979). *Organizational surveys: An internal assessment of organizational health*. Glenview, IL: Scott, Foresman.

Durand, V. M. (1983). Behavioral ecology of a staff incentive program: Effects on absenteeism and resident disruptive behavior. *Behavior Modification, 7*, 165–181.

Durand, V. M. (1986). Employee absenteeism: A selected review of antecedents and consequences. *Journal of Organizational Behavior Management, 7*, 135–167.

Eisenberger, R., Huntington, R., Hutchison, S., & Sowa, D. (1986). Perceived organizational support. *Journal of Applied Psychology, 71*, 500–507.

Ellis, T. E., & Linton, J. C. (1982). Training needs of mental health personnel: A statewide survey. Paper presented at the annual convention of the American Psychological Association (90th, Washington, DC, August 23–27, 1982).

Ewing, L. S. (1967). Fighting and death from stress in the cockroach. *Science, 155*, 1035–1036.

Favell, J. E., Favell, Jas. E., Riddle, J. I., & Risley, T. R. (1984). Promoting change in mental retardation facilities: Getting services from the paper to the people. In W. P. Christian, G. T. Hannah, & T. J. Glahn (Eds.), *Programming effective human services: Strategies for institutional change and client transition* (pp. 15–37). New York: Plenum.

Ferster, C. B., & Skinner, B. F. (1957). *Schedules of reinforcement.* New York: Appleton-Century-Crofts.

Feshbach, S., & Weiner, B. (1986). *Personality.* (2nd Ed.). Lexington, MA: D. C. Heath.

Festinger, L. (1957). *A theory of cognitive dissonance.* Evanston, IL: Row, Peterson.

Fitts, W. H. (1972). *The self concept and performance.* Research Monograph No. 5. Nashville, TN: The Dede Wallace Center.

Ford, J. E. (1981). A simple punishment procedure for controlling employee absenteeism. *Journal of Organizational Behavior Management, 3*, 71–79.

Ford, J. K., & Noe, R. A. (1987). Self-assessed training needs: The effects of attitudes toward training, managerial level, and function. *Personnel Psychology, 40*, 39–53.

Fox, D. H., & Fox, R. T. (1984). Why strategic planning for nursing? In J. M. Virgo (Ed.), *Health care: An international perspective.* Edwardsville, IL: International Health Economics and Management at Southern Illinois University.

Frederiksen, L. W. (1982). Organizational behavior management: An overview. In L. W. Frederiksen (Ed.), *Handbook of organizational behavior management* (pp. 3–20). New York: Wiley.

Frederiksen, L. W., & Johnson, R. P. (1981). Organizational behavior management. In M. Hersen, R. M. Eisler, & P. M. Miller (Eds.), *Progress in behavior modification.* New York: Academic Press.

Frederiksen, L. W., & Lovett, S. B. (1980). Inside organizational behavior management: Perspectives on an emerging field. *Journal of Organizational Behavior Management, 2*, 193–203.

Friedman, M., & Rosenman, R. H. (1974). *Type A behavior and your heart.* New York: Knopf.

Fryer, D. (1926). Industrial dissatisfaction. *Industrial Psychology, 1*, 25–29.

Fuchs, V. R. (Ed.). (1969). *Production and productivity in the service industries.* New York: National Bureau of Economic Research.

George, M. J., & Baumeister, A. A. (1981). Employee withdrawal and job satisfaction in community residential facilities for mentally retarded persons. *American Journal of Mental Deficiency, 85*, 639–647.

Georgopoulos, B. S., Mahoney, G. M., & Jones, N. W. (1957). A path-goal approach to productivity. *Journal of Applied Psychology, 41*, 345–353.

Gerhart, B. (1987). How important are dispositional factors as determinants of job satisfaction? Implication for job design and other personnel programs. *Journal of Applied Psychology, 72*(3), 366–373.

Gilbreth, F. B., & Gilbreth, L. M. (1921). First steps in finding the one best way to do work. Paper presented at the annual meeting of the American Society of Mechanical Engineers (New York, December 5–9, 1921).

Glass, G. V., McGaw, B., & Smith, M. L. (1981). *Meta-analysis in social research.* Beverly Hills, CA: Sage.

Goldstein, I. L. (1986). *Training in organizations: Needs assessment, development, and evaluation* (2nd Ed.). Monterey, CA: Brooks Cole.

Golembiewski, R. T., Hilles, R., & Kagno, M. S. (1974). A longitudinal study of flexi-time effects: Some consequences of an OD structural intervention. *Journal of Applied Behavioral Science, 10*, 503–532.

Greenblatt, M., & Levinson, D. J. (1965). Mental hospitals. In B. B. Wolman (Ed.), *Handbook of clinical psychology* (pp. 1343–1359), New York: McGraw-Hill.

Greenhaus, J. H., & Parasuraman, S. (1987). A work-nonwork interactive perspective of stress and its consequences. *Journal of Organizational Behavior Management, 8*(2), 37–60.

Grove, B. A. (1968). Attendance reward plan pays. *Personnel Journal, 47*, 119–120.

Hackman, J. R. (1983). Attributes of organizations and their effects on organization members. In M. D. Dunnette (Ed.), *Handbook of industrial and organizational psychology* (pp. 1065–1123). New York: Wiley.

Hage, J. (1980). *Theories of organizations.* New York: Wiley.

Harris, D. L. (1985). The "H-P Way"—A three-part philosophy emphasizing people. In Y. K. Shetty & V. M. Buehler, *Productivity and quality through people* (pp. 91–93). Westport, CT: Quorum.

Hasenfeld, Y. (1983). *Human service organizations.* Englewood Cliffs, NJ: Prentice-Hall.

Heaton, H. (1977). *Productivity in service organizations.* New York: McGraw-Hill.

Heider, F. (1958). *The psychology of interpersonal relations.* New York: Wiley.

Heiser, K. F., & Wolman, B. B. (1965). Mental deficiencies. In B. B. Wolman (Ed.), *Handbook of clinical psychology* (pp. 838–854). New York: McGraw-Hill.

Herzberg, F. (1959). *The motivation to work* (2nd Ed.). New York: Wiley.

Herzberg, F. (1966). *Work and the nature of man.* Cleveland: World Publishing.

Hilgard, E. R., & Bower, G. H. (1966). *Theories of learning* (3rd Ed). New York: Appleton-Century-Crofts.

Hinkle, A., & Burns, M. (1978). The clinician-executive: A review. *Administration In Mental Health, 6*, 3–21.

Hinrichs, J. R. (1983). Personnel training. In M. D. Dunnette (Ed.), *Handbook of industrial and organizational psychology* (pp. 829–860). New York: Wiley.

Holmes, T. H., & Rahe, R. H. (1967). The social readjustment rating scale. *Journal of Psychosomatic Research, 11*, 213–218.

Hopkins, B. L., & Sears, J. (1982). Managing behavior for productivity. In L. W. Frederiksen (Ed.), *Handbook of organizational behavior management* (pp. 393–424). New York: Wiley.

Hoppock, R. (1935). *Job satisfaction.* New York: Harper.

Hull, C. L. (1952). *A behavior system.* New Haven: Yale University Press.

Hunt, J. W., & Saul, P. N. (1975). The relationship of age, tenure, and job satisfaction in males and females. *Academy of Management Journal, 12*, 690–702.

Hunter, J. E., & Schmidt, F. L. (1982). Fitting people to jobs: The impact of personnel selection on national productivity. In M. D. Dunnett & E. A. Fleishman (Eds.), *Human performance and productivity: Human capability assessment.* Hillsdale, NJ: Erlbaum.

Hunter, J. E., & Schmidt, F. L. (1983). Quantifying the effects of psychological interventions on employee job performance and work-force productivity. *American Psychologist, 38*, 473–478.

Hurrell, J. J., Jr., & Colligan, M. J. (1987). Machine pacing and shiftwork: Evidence for job stress. *Journal of Organizational Behavior Management, 8*(2), 159–175.

Hutchison, J. M., Jarman, P. H., & Bailey, J. S. (1980). Public posting with a habilitation team: Effects on attendance and performance. *Behavior Modification, 4*, 57–70.

Iacocca, L. (1984). *Iacocca: An autobiography.* New York: Bantam.

Ilgen, D. R., & Moore, C. F. (1987). Types and choices of performance feedback. *Journal of Applied Psychology, 72*(3), 401–406.

Ivancevich, J. M., & Matteson, M. T. (1980). *Stress and work: A managerial perspective.* Dallas: Scott, Foresman.

Jackson, S. E. (1983). Participation in decision making as a strategy for reducing job-related strain. *Journal of Applied Psychology, 68*, 3–19.

Jewman, J. E. (1974). Predicting absenteeism and turnover: A field comparison of Fishbein's model and traditional job attitude measures. *Journal of Applied Psychology, 59*, 610–615.

Jones, E. E., & Davis, K. E. (1965). From acts to dispositions: The attribution process in person perception. In L. Berkowitz (Ed.), *Advances in experimental social psychology* (Vol. 2), New York: Academic Press.

Jones, J. W. (1980). *The Staff Burnout Scale for Health Professionals (SBS-HP).* Park Ridge, IL: London House.

Jones, J. W. (1982). Measuring staff burnout. *Technical Report* No. E3, Park Ridge, IL: London House.

Kahn, R. L., Wolfe, D. M., Quinn, R. P., Snock, J. D., & Rosenthal, R. A. (1964). *Organizational stress: Studies in role conflict and ambiguity.* New York: Wiley.

Kalat, J. W. (1984). *Biological psychology* (3rd Ed.). Belmont, CA: Wadsworth.

Katzell, R. A. (1964). Personal values, job satisfaction, and job behavior. In H. Borow (Ed.), *Man in a world of work*. Boston: Houghton-Mifflin.

Katzell, R. A., & Guzzo, R. A. (1983). Psychological approaches to productivity improvement. *American Psychologist, 38,* 468–472.

Kazdin, A. E. (1978). *History of behavior modification*. Baltimore: Baltimore University Press.

Kazdin, A. E. (1984). *Behavior modification in applied settings* (3rd Ed.). Homewood, IL: Dorsey.

Kempen, R. W., & Hail, R. V. (1977). Reduction of institutional absenteeism: Results of a behavioral approach. *Journal of Organizational Behavior Management, 1,* 1–22.

Kets de Vries, M. F. R., & Miller, D. (1984). *The neurotic organization*. San Francisco: Jossey-Bass.

King, A. S. (1976). Training in the health-care field. In R. L. Craig (Ed.), *Training and development handbook* (2nd Ed.) (pp. 29–1 through 29–14). New York: McGraw-Hill.

Komaki, J. (1983). Why we don't reinforce: The issues. *Journal of Organizational Behavior Management, 4*(3/4), 97–100.

Kreitner, R. (1982). Controversy in OBM: History, misconceptions, and ethics. In L. W. Frederiksen (Ed.), *Handbook of organizational behavior management* (pp. 71–91). New York: Wiley.

Landy, F. J. (1985). *Psychology of work behavior* (3rd Ed.). Homewood, IL: Dorsey.

Landy, F. J., Farr, J. L., & Jacobs, R. R. (1982). Utility concepts in performance measurement. *Organizational Behavior and Human Performance, 30,* 15–40.

Landy, F. J., & Trumbo, D. A. (1980). *Psychology of work behavior* (Rev. Ed.). Homewood, IL: Dorsey.

Lawler, E. E. III. (1983). Control systems in organizations. In M. D. Dunnette (Ed.), *Handbook of industrial and organizational psychology* (pp. 1247–1291). New York: Wiley.

Lawler, E. E. III, & Hackman, J. R. (1969). Impact of employee participation in the development of pay incentive plans: A field experiment. *Journal of Applied Psychology, 53,* 467–471.

Lee, C. (1984). Training the Hewlett-Packard Team. *Training, 21*(3), 24–27, 31.

Lewin, K. (1938). *The conceptual representation and the measurement of psychological forces*. Durham, NC: Duke University Press.

Lewin, K. (1951). *Field theory in social science*. New York: Harper and Row.

Linden, F. (1984). Special consumer survey report. (Based on a survey by NFO Research, Inc.). New York: The Conference Board.

Locke, E. A. (1968). Toward a theory of task motivation and incentives. *Organizational Behavior and Human Performance 3,* 157–189.

Locke, E. A. (1970). Job satisfaction and job performance: A theoretical analysis. *Organizational Behavior and Human Performance, 5,* 484–500.

Locke, E. A., Shaw, K. N., Saari, L. M., & Latham, G. P. (1981). Goal-setting and task performance: 1969–1980. *Psychological Bulletin, 90,* 125–152.

Loftquist, L. H., & Dawis, R. V. (1969). *Adjustment to work*. New York: Appleton-Century-Crofts.

McClelland, D. C. (1951). *Personality*. New York: Dryden Press.

McClelland, D. C. (1961). *The achieving society*. Princeton, NJ: Van Nostrand.

McClelland, D. C., Atkinson, J. W., Clark, R. A., & Lowell, E. L. (1953). *The achievement motive*. New York: Appleton-Century-Crofts.

McCormick, E. J., & Ilgen, D. R. (1985). *Industrial and organizational psychology* (8th Ed.). Englewood Cliffs, NJ: Prentice-Hall.

McDougall, W. (1908). *An introduction to social psychology*. London: Methuen and Co.

McGrath, J. E. (1983). Stress and behavior in organizations. In M. D. Dunnette (Ed.), *Handbook of industrial and organizational psychology* (pp. 1351–1395). New York: Wiley.

McGregor, D. (1960). *The human side of enterprise*. New York: McGraw-Hill.

McNamara, R. D. (1986). Forces in the administration of public residential facilities. In J. Thaw & A. J. Cuvo (Eds.), *Developing responsive human resources* (pp. 51–82). Hillsdale, NJ: Erlbaum Associates.

Markham, S. E., Dansereau, F., & Alutto, J. A. (1982). Group size and absenteeism rates: A longitudinal analysis. *Academy of Management Journal, 25*, 921–927.

Martin, W. T. (1987). Motivation and productivity in human service organizations in the United States. Unpublished report. Author.

Maslach, C. (1976). Burned-out. *Human Behavior*. September, 1976, 16–22.

Maslach, C. (1978). Job burnout: How people cope. *Public Welfare, 36*, 56–58.

Maslach, C., & Jackson, S. (1981). *The Maslach Burnout Inventory*. Palo Alto, CA: Consulting Psychologists Press.

Maslow, A. H. (1954). *Motivation and personality*. New York: Harper & Row.

Matsui, T., Okada, A., & Inoshita, O. (1983). Mechanism of feedback affecting task performance. *Organizational Behavior and Human Performance, 31*, 114–122.

Matteson, M. T., & Ivancevich, J. M. (1982). The how, what and why of stress management training. *Personnel Journal, 61* (10), 768–774.

Mechanic, D. (1973). The sociology of organizations. In S. Feldman (Ed.), *The administration of mental health services* (pp. 138–166). Springfield, IL: Thomas.

Meyer, M. C. (1978). Demotivation—Its causes and cure. *Personnel Journal, 57*(5), 260–266.

Miner, J. B. (1963). *The management of ineffective performance*. New York: McGraw-Hill.

Miner, J. B. (1966). *Introduction to industrial clinical psychology*. New York: McGraw-Hill.

Miner, J. B. (1975). *The challenge of managing*. Philadelphia: Saunders.

Miner, J. B., & Brewer, J. F. (1983). The management of ineffective performance. In M. D. Dunnette (Ed.), *Handbook of industrial and organizational psychology* (pp. 995–1029). New York: Wiley.

Mintzberg, H. (1979). *The structuring of organizations*. Englewood Cliffs, NJ: Prentice-Hall.

Mintzberg, H. (1981). Organizational design: Fashion or fit? *Harvard Business Review*, 103–116.

Morgan, B., Holmes, G. E., & Bundy, C. E. (1976). *Methods in adult education* (3rd Ed.). Danville, IL: The Interstate Printers & Publishers.

Mowday, R., Porter, L., & Steers, R. (1982). *Organizational linkages: The psychology of commitment, absenteeism, and turnover.* New York: Academic Press.

Munsterberg, H. (1913). *Psychology and industrial efficiency.* Boston: Houghton-Mifflin.

Murray, H. A. (1938). *Explorations in personality: A clinical and experimental study of fifty men of college age.* New York: Oxford University Press.

Naisbitt, J. (1984). *Megatrends.* New York: Warner Books.

NIMH. (1983). *Mental health, United States 1983.* Rockville, MD: United States Department of Health and Human Services, NIMH.

NIMH. (1985). *Mental health directory.* Rockville, MD: United States Department of Health and Human Services, NIMH.

NIMH. (1986). *Directory of programs and facilities for mentally retarded offenders.* Rockville, MD: United States Department of Health and Human Services, NIMH.

Oldham, G. R., & Fried, Y. (1987). Employee reactions to workspace characteristics. *Journal of Applied Psychology, 72*(1), 75–80.

O'Reilly, C. III., & Chatman, J. (1986). Organizational commitment and psychological attachment: The effects of compliance, identification, and internalization of prosocial behavior. *Journal of Applied Psychology, 71,* 492–499.

Organ, D. W., & Hamner, W. C. (1982). *Organizational behavior: An applied psychological approach* (Rev. Ed.). Plano, TX: Business Publications, Inc.

Ouchi, W. G. (1981). *Theory Z: How American business can meet the Japanese challenge.* New York: Avon.

Ouchi, W. G. (1985). Productivity through changed business/government relationships: A modern model. In Y. K. Shetty & V. M. Buehler (Eds.), *Productivity and quality through people* (pp. 288–311). Westport, CT: Quorum.

Packard, D. (1974). Lessons of leadership: David Packard. *Nation's Business* (January), 42.

Parkinson, C. N. (1957). *Parkinson's Law.* Boston: Houghton Mifflin.

Peter, L. J., & Hull, R. (1969). *The Peter Principle: Why things always go wrong.* New York: Morrow.

Peters, T. J., & Waterman, R. H., Jr. (1982). *In search of excellence.* New York: Harper & Row.

Pierce, P. S., Hoffman, J. L., & Pelletier, L. P. (1974). The 4-day work week versus the 5-day work week: Comparative use of sick time and overtime by direct care personnel in an institutional facility for the severely and profoundly mentally retarded. *Mental Retardation, 12,* 22–24.

Pines, A., & Aronson, E. (1981). *Burnout: From tedium to personal growth.* New York: The Free Press.

Porter, L. W., & Lawler, E. E. (1968). *Managerial attitudes and performance.* Homewood, IL: Dorsey.

Porter, L. W., & Steers, R. M. (1973). Organizational, work and personal factors in employee turnover and absenteeism. *Psychological Bulletin, 80*, 151–176.

Porter, L. W., Steers, R. M., Mowday, R., & Boulian, P. (1974). Organizational commitment, job satisfaction, and turnover among psychiatric technicians. *Journal of Applied Psychology, 59*, 603–609.

Price, J. L. (1977). *The study of turnover.* Ames: Iowa University Press.

Prue, D. M. (1981). Performance feedback in organizational behavior management: A review. *Journal of Organizational Behavior Management, 3*, 1–16.

Rabinowitz, S., & Hall, D. (1977). Organizational research on job involvement. *Psychological Bulletin, 84*, 265–288.

Reichers, A. E. (1986). Conflict and organizational commitments. *Journal of Applied Psychology, 71*, 508–514.

Reid, D. H., Schuh-Wear, C. L., & Brannon, M. E. (1978). Use of a group contingency to decrease staff absenteeism in a state institution. *Behavior Modification, 2*, 251–266.

Reid, D. H., & Shoemaker, J. (1984). Behavioral supervision: Methods of improving institutional staff performance. In W. P. Christian, G. T. Hannah, and T. J. Glahn (Eds.), *Programming effective human services* (pp. 39–61). New York: Plenum.

Reid, D. H., & Whitman, T. L. (1983). Behavioral staff management in institutions: A critical review of effectiveness and acceptability. *Analysis and Intervention in Developmental Disabilities, 3*, 131–149.

Riley, A. W., & Frederiksen, L. W. (1984). Organizational behavior management in human service settings: Problems and prospects. *Journal of Organizational Behavior Management, 5*, 3–16.

Roe, A. (1956). *The psychology of occupations.* New York: Wiley.

Roethlisberger, F.J., & Dickson, W. J. (1939). *Management and the worker.* Cambridge, MA: Harvard University Press.

Rollins, F. H. (1985). Delta's teamwork approach to labor/management relations. In Y. K. Shetty & V. M. Buehler (Eds.), *Productivity and quality through people* (pp. 129–132). Westport, CT: Quorum.

Rollins, T. (1987). Compensation: Pay for performance: The pros and cons. *Personnel Journal, 66*(6), 104, 106, 111.

Ross, P. C. (1982). Training: Behavior change and the improvement of business performance. In L. W. Frederiksen (Ed.), *Handbook of organizational behavior management* (pp. 181–217). New York: Wiley.

Rotter, J. B. (1966). Generalized expectancies for internal versus external control of reinforcements. *Psychological Monographs, 80*(1), Whole No. 609).

Rotter, N. G., & Mills, M. K. (1982). The relationship between organizational commitment, intention to remain and attitude towards absenteeism. Paper presented at the annual meeting of the Eastern Psychological Association (53rd, Baltimore, MD, April 15–18, 1982).

Rowland, D. C., & Greene, B. (1987). Incentive pay: Productivity's own reward. *Personnel Journal, 66*(6), 48–57.

Ryan, T. A. (1970). *International behavior.* New York: Ronald Press.

Sarata, B. (1975). Employees' satisfaction in agencies serving retarded persons. *American Journal of Mental Deficiency, 79*, 434–442.

Schaffer, R. H. (1953). Job satisfaction as related to need satisfaction in work. *Psychological Monographs, 67* (Whole No. 364).

Schlenker, J. A., & Gutek, B. A. (1987). Effects of role loss on work-related attitudes. *Journal of Applied Psychology, 72*(2), 287–293.

Schmidt, F. L., Hunter, J. E., McKenzie, R. C., & Muldrow, T. W. (1979). Impact of valid selection procedures on work-force productivity. *Journal of Applied Psychology, 64*, 609–626.

Schmidt, F. L., Hunter, J. E., & Pearlman, K. (1982). Assessing the economic impact of personnel programs on workforce productivity. *Personnel Psychology, 35*, 333–348.

Schmitz, L. M., & Henemann, H. G. III. (1980). Do positive reinforcement programs reduce employee absenteeism? *Personnel Administrator* (September), 87–93.

Schwartz, G. G., & Neikirk, W. (1983). *The work revolution.* New York: Rawson Associates.

Searls, D. J., Bravelt, G. N., & Miskimins, R. W. (1974). Work values of the chronically unemployed. *Journal of Applied Psychology, 59*, 93–95.

Seligman, M. E. P. (1975). *Helplessness: On depression, development, and death.* San Francisco: Freeman.

Selye, H. (1956). *The stress of life.* New York: McGraw-Hill.

Seybolt, J. W. (1976). Work satisfaction as a function of the person-environment interaction. *Organizational Behavior And Human Performance, 17*, 66–75.

Shetty, Y. K., & Buehler, V. M. (1985). *Productivity and quality through people.* Westport, CT: Quorum.

Shoemaker, J., & Reid, D. H. (1980). Decreasing chronic absenteeism among institutional staff: Effects of a low-cost attendance program. *Journal of Organizational Behavior Management, 2*, 317–328.

Siegel, L., & Lane, I. M. (1982). *Personnel and organizational psychology.* Homewood, IL: Irwin.

Siropolis, N. C. (1982). *Small business management: A guide to entrepreneurship* (2nd Ed.). Boston: Houghton Mifflin.

Skinner, B. F. (1938). *The behavior of organisms: An experimental analysis.* New York: Appleton-Century-Crofts.

Skinner, B. F. (1953). *Science and human behavior.* New York: Free Press.

Skinner, B.F. (1969). *Contingencies of reinforcement: A theoretical analysis.* Englewood Cliffs, NJ: Prentice-Hall.

Skinner, B. F. (1974). *About behaviorism.* New York: Knopf.

Sluyter, G. V. (1976). The unit management system: Anatomy of structural change. *Mental Retardation, 14*, 14–16.

Sluyter, G. V., & Mukherjee, A. K. (1986). Validation of a job satisfaction instrument for residential-care employees. *Mental Retardation, 24*, 223–227.

Sluyter, G. V., Mukherjee, A. K., & Hinkle, D. E. (1985). Job satisfaction among residential care employees: A factor-analytic study. *Superintendents Digest, 4*, 15–19.

Smith, P. C., Kendall, L. M., & Hulin, C. L. (1969). *The measurement of satisfaction in work and retirement: A strategy for the study of attitudes.* Chicago: Rand-McNally.

Sproull, L. S., & Hofmeister, K. R. (1986). Thinking about implementation. *Journal of Management, 12*(1), 43–60.

Stanton, E. S. (1983). A critical reevaluation of motivation, management, and productivity. *Personnel Journal, 62*(3), 208–214.

Steers, R. M., & Rhodes, S. R. (1978). Major influences on employee attendance: A process model. *Journal of Applied Psychology, 63*, 391–407.

Steinmetz, L. L. (1969). *Managing the Marginal and Unsatisfactory Performer.* Reading, MA: Addison-Wesley.

Taylor, F. W. (1903). Shop management. *Transactions of the American Society of Mechanical Engineers, 24*, 1337–1481.

Taylor, F. W. (1911). *The principles of scientific management.* New York: Harper.

Taylor, H. C., & Russell, J. T. (1939). The relationship of validity coefficients to the practical effectiveness of tests in selection. *Journal of Applied Psychology, 23*, 565–578.

Thaw, J., Benjamin, E., & Cuvo, A. J. (1986). The professionals: Difficulties and directions. In J. Thaw & A. J. Cuvo (Eds.). *Developing responsive human services* (pp. 149–189). Hillsdale, NJ: Erlbaum Associates.

Thaw, J., & Cuvo, A. J. (Eds.). (1986). *Developing responsive human services.* Hillsdale, NJ: Erlbaum Associates.

Thaw, J., & Wolfe, S. F. (1986). The direct-care worker: A socio-cultural analysis. In J. Thaw and A. J. Cuvo (Eds.), *Developing responsive human services* (pp. 83–147).

Thompson, V. A. (1976). *Bureaucracy and the modern world.* Morristown, NJ: General Learning Press.

Thorndike, E. L. (1932). *The fundamentals of learning.* New York: Teachers College, Columbia University.

Thorne, G. D., & Thaw, J. (1986). Policy and the perspective of state government. In J. Thaw & A. J. Cuvo (Eds.), *Developing responsive human services* (pp. 229–260). Hillsdale, NJ: Erlbaum Associates.

Toffler, A. (1970). *Future shock.* New York: Random House.

Tolman, E. C. (1932). *Purposive behavior in animals and man.* New York: Century.

Tosi, H. L., & Hamner, W. C. (Eds.). (1974). *Organizational behavior and human performance: A contingency approach.* Chicago: St. Clair Press.

Tredgold, A. F. (1952). *A textbook of mental deficiency* (8th Ed.). Baltimore: Williams & Wilkins.

Triandis, H. C., Felden, J., Weldon, D. E., & Harvey, W. M. (1975). Ecosystem distrust and the hard-to-employ. *Journal of Applied Psychology, 60*, 44–56.

Turkington, C. (1985). "Having it all" leads to burnout. *APA Monitor, 16*(11), 13.

Tuttle, T. C. (1983). Organizational productivity: A challenge for psychologists. *American Psychologist, 38*, 479–486.

Vinton, D. (1987). Delegation for employee development. *Training and Development Journal, 41*, 65–67.

Virgo, J. M. (1984). Decision making in the regulatory system. In J. M. Virgo (Ed.), *Health care: an international perspective*. Edwardsville, IL: International Health Economics and Management at Southern Illinois University.

Vollmer, H. M., & Kinney, J. A. (1955). Age, education and job satisfaction. *Personnel, 32*, 38–43.

Vroom, V. H. (1964). *Work and motivation*. New York: Wiley.

Wallin, J. A., & Johnson, R. D. (1976). The positive reinforcement approach to controlling employee absenteeism. *Personnel Journal, 55*, 390–392.

Watson, D., Pennebaker, J. W., & Folger, R. (1987). Beyond negative affectivity: Measuring stress and satisfaction in the workplace. In J. M. Ivancevich and D. C. Ganster (Eds.), Job stress: From theory to suggestion (pp. 5–18) *Journal of Organizational Behavior Management, 8* (Whole No. 2).

Weaver, C. N. (1980). Job satisfaction in the United States in the 1970s. *Journal of Applied Psychology, 65*, 364–367.

Webber, R. A. (1979). *Management: Basic elements of managing organizations* (Rev. Ed.). Homewood, IL: Irwin.

Weber, M. (1947). *The theory of social and economic organizations*, translated by A. M. Henderson and Talcott Parsons. New York: Macmillan.

Weekely, J. A., Blake, F., O'Connor, E. J., & Peters, L. H. (1985). A comparison of three methods of estimating the standard deviation of performance in dollars. *Journal of Applied Psychology, 70*(1), 122–126.

Wehrenberg, S. B. (1987). Supervisors as trainers: The long-term gains of OJT. *Personnel Journal, 66*(4), 48, 50–51.

Weick, K. E. (1979). *The social psychology of organizations* (2nd Ed.). Reading, MA: Addison-Wesley.

Wexley, K. N., & Latham, G. P. (1981). *Developing and training human resources in organizations*. Glenview, IL: Scott, Foresman.

Wittenborn, J. R. (1965). Depression. In B. B. Wolman (Ed.), *Handbook of clinical psychology* (pp. 1030–1057). New York: McGraw-Hill.

Wood, C. T. (1984). Productivity in health care. In J. M. Virgo (Ed.), *Health care: An international perspective*. Edwardsville, IL: International Health Economics and Management at Southern Illinois University.

Woodworth, R. S. (1918). *Dynamic psychology*. New York: Columbia University Press.

Zaharia, E. S., & Baumeister, A. A. (1978). Cross-organizational job satisfaction of technician level staff members. *American Journal of Mental Deficiency, 84*, 30–35.

Ziarnik, J. P., & Bernstein, G. S. (1982). A critical examination of the effect of inservice training on staff performance. *Mental Retardation, 20*(3), 109–114.

INDEX

ABOUT THE AUTHOR

WILLIAM T. MARTIN was formerly a Social Services Administrator at Winfield State Hospital and Training Center. He has also held psychology and administrative positions at a hospital as well as worked in psychology at a community mental health center and in mental retardation. He has been a college faculty member in psychology and human resource management.